THE TAO of
ENRON

THE TAO of ENRON

SPIRITUAL LESSONS from a FORTUNE 500 FALLOUT

CHRIS SEAY
WITH CONTRIBUTING AUTHOR **CHRIS BRYAN**

NAVPRESS

Bringing Truth to Life
P.O. Box 35001, Colorado Springs, Colorado 80935

OUR GUARANTEE TO YOU

We believe so strongly in the message of our books that
we are making this quality guarantee to you. If for any
reason you are disappointed with the content of this
book, return the title page to us with your name and
address and we will refund to you the list price of the
book. To help us serve you better, please briefly describe
why you were disappointed. Mail your refund request to:
NavPress, P.O. Box 35002, Colorado Springs, CO 80935.

The Navigators is an international Christian organization. Our mission is to reach, disciple, and equip
people to know Christ and to make Him known through successive generations. We envision multitudes
of diverse people in the United States and every other nation who have a passionate love for Christ, live a
lifestyle of sharing Christ's love, and multiply spiritual laborers among those without Christ.

NavPress is the publishing ministry of The Navigators. NavPress publications help believers learn
biblical truth and apply what they learn to their lives and ministries. Our mission is to stimulate
spiritual formation among our readers.

ISBN 1-57683-433-6

Cover Design: David Carlson Design
Cover Image: Clay Patrick McBride/Photonica
Creative Team: Jay Howver, Steve Halliday, Darla Hightower, Nat Akin, Don Simpson, Glynese Northam

Some of the anecdotal illustrations in this book are true to life and are included with the permission
of the persons involved. All other illustrations are composites of real situations, and any resemblance
to people living or dead is coincidental.

Unless otherwise identified, all Scripture quotations in this publication are taken from the HOLY
BIBLE: NEW INTERNATIONAL VERSION® (NIV®). Copyright © 1973, 1978, 1984 by
International Bible Society. Used by permission of Zondervan Publishing House. All rights reserved.
Other versions used include: the New American Standard Bible (NASB), © The Lockman Foundation
1960, 1962, 1963, 1968, 1971, 1972, 1973, 1975, 1977; THE MESSAGE (MSG). Copyright ©
1993, 1994, 1995, 1996, 2000, 2001, 2002. Used by permission of NavPress Publishing Group; the
Holy Bible, New Living Translation, (NLT) copyright © 1996. Used by permission of Tyndale House
Publishers, Inc., Wheaton, Illinois 60189. All rights reserved; and the King James Version (KJV).

Seay, Chris.
  The Tao of Enron : spiritual lessons from a Fortune 500 fallout /
Chris Seay.
    p. cm.
Includes bibliographical references.
  ISBN 1-57683-433-6
  1. Capitalism--Religious aspects--Christianity. 2. Enron
Corp.--Corrupt practices. I. Title.
  BR115.C3 S49 2002
  261.8'5--dc21   2002153486

Printed in the United States of America
1 2 3 4 5 6 7 8 9 10 / 07 06 05 04 02

FOR A FREE CATALOG OF
NAVPRESS BOOKS & BIBLE STUDIES,
CALL 1-800-366-7788 (USA)
OR 1-416-499-4615 (CANADA)

This book is dedicated to the children of my family who will carry forward this legacy. I pray your lives embody the kind of honesty, integrity, compassion, and love that we strive for in this book. To: Olivia, Phillip, Natalie, Baby Seay, Emma, Jaxson, Ethan Cade, Silas, Hanna Shalom, Trinity Salem, and Baby Solomon. I love you all!

To the children I am privileged to love, teach, and pastor: Chandler, Andrea, Jack, Harry, Wilson, Zane, Zoe, Noah, Reece, Aimee, Asher Dean, Jade, Baby Owens, River, Rocco, Isaiah, Baby Hartley, Max, Ethan, Kelsey, Matt, Aliah, Blake, Baby Burlton, Clyde, David, Dylan, Baby Johnson, Noah, Emma, Joseph, and beautiful Arabella. There are and will be many other children; I pray we will show them the right path with love and patience.

CONTENTS

ACKNOWLEDGMENTS   **9**

INTRODUCTION: Trading Wealth for Abundance   **11**
1. Capitalism Run Amok   **17**
2. An Era of Infectious Greed   **27**
3. Kenneth Lay: Crooked, Clueless, or Consumed
   by a Fast-Paced Culture?   **41**
4. The Disaster of Dualism   **49**
5. Jeff Skilling: Unbreakable   **65**
6. Boast Only in the "E"   **71**
7. Rebecca Mark: Rise to the Top   **79**
8. A Lust for Power   **85**
9. Andrew Fastow: A Portrait of Impatience   **93**
10. I Want It Now   **99**
11. Sherron Watkins: A Lesson in True Faith   **115**
12. The Fatal Flaw of the Western World   **123**
13. J. Clifford Baxter: Life Is Fleeting   **137**
14. Chris Bryan: Willing to Walk Away   **143**
15. On Trial in the Court of the Creator   **151**
16. The Antidote to Affluenza   **161**

EPILOGUE: In Search of an Honorable and Satisfying Life   **173**

AFTERWORD TO CHURCH LEADERS:
    McFaith: The Gospel at 50 Percent Off   **179**

DISCUSSION QUESTIONS   **183**

APPENDIX: A Few Suggestions for Simple Living   **191**

ENDNOTES   **197**

ABOUT THE AUTHORS   **207**

Lisa, you are the love of my life—thank you for making me a better person. Mom, Dad, Brian, Robbie, Jen, and Jessica—I love you. Ruth, your love and support allow me the time to do this. Justin Hyde, my padawan apprentice, it is always a joy engaging the creative process together. Greg Garrett, you are helping me become a better writer; your friendship and insight is invaluable. James Christopher Bryan, you are a kind, gentle, and loving man, and this book would not have been possible without your significant contribution.

Thanks to all the Enron employees who willingly shared their knowledge, insight, and stories.

To Ecclesia, my community and fellow journeyers—the elders, staff, and deacons have worked and sacrificed to make this book a reality. Thank you!

Emergent and the Emergent Senior Fellows, YS, UBA, Acts 29, and BGCT—thanks for your love, friendship, and support.

To all the hardworking folks at NavPress—thanks for doing what it takes to make this book happen so quickly. To Jay Howver, Dan Rich, Terry Behimer, Toben Heim, Sarah Snelling, and Kent Wilson—working with all of you has been a pleasure from beginning to end. The ways of our Creator remain a beautiful enigma.

To the Master, Steve Halliday—you are a wonderful editor. I look forward to more time together.

Trading Wealth for Abundance

Tao: a universal, regarded as an ideal attained to a greater or
lesser degree by those embodying it

The story is bigger than Enron. It is the way of WorldCom. The path
of Global Crossing. The tragedy of Tyco. And the life and eventual
death of all those who would follow in their footsteps.

"The Tao" is an eastern term designed to encompass the whole. In
fact, the Chinese translation of the Bible begins the gospel of John with
"In the beginning was the Tao, and the Tao was with God, and the Tao
was God." Translators thus linked the Chinese term "the tao" with the
Greek term "the logos" (usually rendered into English as "the Word").

So what was "the way" of Enron? What did its top leaders consider the ideal way of doing business? What can we learn from it?

In this book we will trace the path of the now-infamous corporation named Enron so that it might shed light on our own personal
journeys. But finding "the right way" is not easy. In fact, Jesus said
that many will follow the wide path, but the path to life is narrow and

hard to find.[1] We will have to surmount obstacles along the way—but it is possible that as people seeking a genuine faith, we may chart a new course that leads to fulfillment, peace, joy, and justice.

I invite you on this journey, not only through the ruins of this once-ballyhooed but now reviled corporation, but to a place of introspection. The same problems that exist in corporate America even now play out in our own lives and families. Consider Enron as a chief example of "what went wrong" and thus a parable that may lead us to what is right.

A CULTURE BUILT ON GREED

Media reports continue to paint an ugly portrait of an entire corporate culture built on rapacious greed. With zero regard for how their aggressively self-obsessed and often immoral actions would bankrupt the retirement and investment portfolios of thousands of investors (and put thousands of then-unknowing employees out of work), key executives at Enron enriched themselves through a complicated series of sham corporations and highly suspect accounting procedures. What happened at Enron leads us to question our own trust in humanity and our expectations of the future.

Yet I am convinced that 99.9 percent of Enron employees are basically honest and fine people—and I include the former chairman in that group, despite the late-night comedians who have found in this corporate implosion a fresh source of material. Jay Leno joked, "This past Sunday, former Enron CEO Ken Lay went to a church in Houston. On the way out, a reporter asked him how he thought it was going to work out. Lay said, 'With God's help we'll get through it.' To which the devil said, 'Hey, I thought we had a deal.'"

We live in strange days. The kings have become paupers and the paupers have lost all hope. As a Houstonian, I felt the sting of the incineration of our city's largest employer. My hometown has seen hard times: the oil bust of the 1980s, massive hurricanes, the loss of the beloved Houston Oilers (and their not-so-beloved owner), and now the implosion of a corporation that promised a bright economic future. Friends of mine lost their jobs and their life savings in the collapse. I see in this story echoes of the devastation described in the book of Revelation: "They threw dust on their heads and cried as if the world had come to an end: 'Doom, doom, the great city doomed! All who owned ships or did business by sea got rich on her getting and spending. And now it's over—wiped out in one hour!'"[2]

But this Enron fallout appears different from the other trials faced by our Texas town, now the fourth largest city in the U.S. It destroys a common assumption that man is basically good and warns us that a diseased form of capitalism feeds on corruption and greed and almost certainly leads to the collapse of personal ethics. The survival of the fittest means that someone else must suffer for our gain.

These unforeseen economic failures have turned the world upside down; even expected events have become unpredictable. Take one recent incident as an example. Many times I have seen a homeless man hovering about my neighborhood gas station, darting to a luxury SUV in the hopes of snaring a dollar. I've come to expect the routine. The Rolex-clad businessman will either oblige him or dismiss him.

But not the other day. Instead, I watched a solemn man in a tailored suit berate this clueless wanderer. Screaming with violent fervor, he shouted, "You want to take something from *me*? They have already taken everything. I have nothing left; soon they will take my car. So back the hell up!" The hungry vagrant hadn't bargained on this, so he stepped away quickly, more in disbelief than fear.

Many unsuspecting strangers have absorbed the venom of deflated ex-Enroners. The seemingly untouchable rich have reached their wits' end.

The second largest bankruptcy in American history offers us more than a lesson in economics. It speaks into the American lifestyle and critiques our core values. We should consider this a wake-up call, a warning that our Eurocentric version of capitalism is insolvent. King Solomon has a word for all those who allow themselves to fall prey to the seduction of wealth:

> The one who loves money is never satisfied with money, nor the one who loves wealth with big profits. More smoke. The more loot you get, the more looters show up. And what fun is that—to be robbed in broad daylight? Hard and honest work earns a good night's sleep, whether supper is beans or steak. But a rich man's belly gives him insomnia. Here's a piece of bad luck I've seen happen: A man hoards far more wealth than is good for him and then loses it all in a bad business deal. He fathered a child but hasn't a cent left to give him. He arrived naked from the womb of his mother; he'll leave in the same condition—with nothing. This is bad luck, for sure—naked he came, naked he went. So what was the point of working for a salary of smoke? All for a miserable life spent in the dark?[3]

Many Enron employees have asked me, "As you have studied the company, what do you think happened at Enron?" I usually describe a permissive culture focused solely on profits, a company that leveraged enormous and unmanageable debt in an effort to create wealth, a corporation that tried to hide its debt in shady partnerships. This cycle, I say, led inevitably to Enron's demise. And I ask, did Enron executives do anything illegal? The courts have yet to speak. But who can doubt that the company ventured into the catastrophically *immoral*?

When I speak like this, many insiders stare back and counsel me, "Focus more on Skilling" or "Concentrate on Fastow." And I have to admit: if we were seeking a place to lay blame, they might be pointing in the right direction. *The Tao of Enron*, however, is not about fixing blame. Instead it encourages us to look past the infamous figures at Enron to the real causes of the corporate collapse. Our journey together will take us not only through the bare facts of a devastating bankruptcy, but into a place where we can peer into our own souls and find redemption in a story filled with brokenness and greed.

The Tao of Enron shows how the *actual* core values at Enron— not the ones loudly appearing in the company's PR materials—led inevitably to its implosion. By sketching out the stories of several of the principal players—including Jeff Skilling, Rebecca Mark, Andrew Fastow, and Ken Lay—I try to show how pride, impatience, a lust for power, and the ability to mentally separate issues of faith from the practice of business joined forces to destroy one of America's most admired "young" companies.

But again, this is not merely another accounting of the Enron disaster. This book provides a clear warning to businesspeople who even now stand but one step away from the same deadly trap that pulverized Enron. All of us must choose between two roads that stretch out before us—and all of us are "this close" to striding down the darker one. We cannot allow ourselves to be destroyed by the things that we most desire. For good reason Scripture declares, "Your greedy luxuries are a cancer in your gut, destroying your life from within. You thought you were piling up wealth. What you've piled up is judgment."[4]

So is it possible to choose well? Is it possible to walk down the right road, despite the overwhelming pressures that seek to turn us the other way? In the chapters to come we will see the answer is a resounding "Yes!" It is my profound hope that the spiritual lessons hidden in this parable will set us all toward lives filled with true abundance—and that means far more than the mere accumulation of wealth.

CHAPTER 1

Capitalism Run Amok

It had been raining all day. The damp air left my skin wet, yet my mouth felt dry and parched. Why? This afternoon I would find myself at the epicenter of the Enron debacle, sharing a cup of coffee with Ken Lay, the former CEO and chairman of the board of Enron Corp.

We met at Lay's diminutive twelfth floor corner office in Houston's River Oaks Bank building. Lay's daughter/attorney, Elizabeth, and spokesperson, Kelly Kimberly, accompanied him. We sat around a large table with the man some would call the most hated man in America and for half an hour talked about the gospel. I also asked him about his family.

"The family's never been closer," he replied. "The family's faith has never been stronger." We talked about prayer and forgiveness and family and the meaning of life and the sovereignty of God. And Ken articulated the stark reality that it's hard to go through something this difficult without faith. He explains with conviction that faith is what sustains him.

After our meeting, I wondered, *Does it make sense for a man in the twilight of his life to destroy the company he created, wipe out his legacy, and spend the rest of his years defending his family against lawsuits? Is this the doing of Ken Lay?* And I answered, no.

But was it his responsibility? Now, that's a different question. As of September 19, 2002, Ken was facing 125 lawsuits—and the number continues to mount every day.

Ken shows all the signs of a man in crisis. His brow wrinkles, his eyes rest behind dark circles, he speaks cautiously—and yet he is the same charismatic leader who compels those still around him to follow him and believe they will succeed. Though some employees have chosen to take Lay to court, others confess a continued loyalty to this man whom they believe was duped by unscrupulous underlings. One Enron executive I know personally says, "I would work for Ken Lay again. I still believe in the man."

When I compared Ken's previous year to the tragic story of Job, he said, "I still have my wife and my children. They haven't left me." And he says it with sincere gratitude, for they all have paid a hefty price.

Ken admits that there are forks in the road, and neither I nor anyone else on this earth knows where the road will take Ken Lay. Many would like to see him in jail. In fact, California Attorney General Bill Lockyer said, "I would love to personally escort Lay to an 8 by 10 cell that he could share with a tattooed dude who says, 'Hi, my name is Spike, honey.'" It is strange to hear such strong rhetoric from an attorney general when Lay has not yet been charged with a crime, but this is the tone in the fallout from Enron.

For years Lay had been moving toward his own plans for retirement when his corporate exit got sidetracked by Jeff Skilling's resignation as CEO. No doubt Lay's family would like for him to simply be a father and grandfather again instead of a man plagued by scandal. As a family they are clearly searching for peace amidst the storm.

Yet many others face their own ferocious storms—and most of them do not enjoy the luxury of anything like Ken Lay's River Oaks mansion and protected millions. They must turn into the howling winds without such comforts.

IT DIDN'T WORK OUT

For ten years, Wayne Stevens, sixty-one, worked for Portland General Electric, a subsidiary of Enron. He retired in January of 2001 from his job as a serviceman at the Trojan Nuclear Plant in Rainier, Oregon. His job involved dismantling and decommissioning radioactive pipes and pumps—slow and careful labor.

Stevens' wife, Katherine, still works for PGE, as she has for the past seventeen years. Before the company's collapse, the couple owned stock worth over $700,000. They held on to the stock even after the first waves of tough times hit and Enron disclosed a loss of about $500 million. They believed in the company. "What's a half-billion dollars to a $70 billion company?" they asked.[1]

Even if they had wanted to sell, though, they couldn't have done so because of the company "lockout." From mid-October to late November, Enron employees found themselves unable to access their accounts. Enron said it was in the process of changing 401K managers, and thus had frozen the assets. But during that period, the stock plummeted from about $32 a share to $9.06, and by November 29 it had dropped to thirty-six cents. It lost 99 percent of its value as investors abandoned ship en masse. The freeze began to look less like procedural bureaucracy than a conspiracy to keep employees from joining the exodus. Since then, hundreds of angry investors have joined a class-action lawsuit to look into the legality of the lockout; the plaintiffs include dozens of PGE employees.

The experience at PGE helps to explain why the Enron debacle has so devastated employee investors. On average, PGE employees invested 62 percent of their portfolios in Enron stock, according to one estimate. The Stevenses sold or rolled over most of their stock at thirty-three cents a share.

"We were like most of the people here," said Wayne Stevens. "For years the media had been saying how great a company this was, one of the jewels of the energy business. You know . . . we just believed them. Even now, I still think [Enron is] going to come back," he said, paused, and then declared, "I don't know why I keep thinking that."[2]

Stevens describes himself as conservative and admits to getting excited when his stock began to rise. "When Enron bought PGE, the stock went through the roof," he said, "and like everybody else we got excited, but we were careful. A lot of friends around us were putting everything into Enron stock. They were making money hand over fist. We had most of our money in mutual funds. But then we moved it over to Enron stock too. We put everything in one basket. We know that you shouldn't do that. But once we did it, we never moved. We were pumping money into it the last couple of years, putting the max that the law would allow, buying stock on the side, out of our own pockets, all thinking of the future, that this money would keep us from having to sell our land. We wanted to save that for our kids. . . . You never dreamed [Enron would] ever go bankrupt."[3]

The Stevens clan planned to use their money to keep their land, twenty-four acres settled by Stevens' grandparents, who traveled from Michigan in 1901. "That's 101 years in the family," said Stevens. "I grew up on this land from the time I was nine years old, and I have so many memories of it, every inch of this ground. I've got myself in this land. We wanted to leave it to our kids, so they'd leave it to their kids, and it would carry on in the family name. But it didn't work out."[4]

GETTING EMOTIONAL

Janice Farmer, a sixty-one-year-old Florida widow, got very emotional while testifying at a U.S. Senate Commerce, Science, and Transportation Committee hearing on the Enron disaster. She described the plunge of her $700,000 retirement fund (built up over sixteen years) to $24,000 during Enron's speedy collapse. Her daughter accompanied her to the hearing to support and help her through her testimony.

"I cannot help but feel that I and thousands of employees like me have been lied to and cheated," Farmer told the senators. "I trusted the management of Enron with my life savings. Senators, I won't mince words here. They betrayed that trust."[5]

Farmer finds comfort in the only retirement support she can count on; in one year she will begin receiving monthly checks from Social Security. "It is extremely important for seniors to know they've got Social Security," said Farmer in a telephone interview from her home in Orlando. "I'm very thankful that Social Security is in my future."[6]

For now, Farmer is making ends meet by counting on a $63 monthly pension check from a previous employer. "Retirement wasn't supposed to be like this," she said. "This wasn't what Enron, America's genius energy supplier, had promised."[7]

Farmer told the senators that she had felt proud to invest in Enron stock. "We were a loyal and hardworking group of employees," she said. "We lived, ate, slept, and breathed Enron because we were owners of the company. I trusted the management of Enron with my life savings."[8]

Eventually she said she became concerned over the stock's slide and called on October 22 to sell her shares, but was told she had been locked out. Farmer was not permitted to sell her stock until November 26 and therefore lost hundreds of thousands of dollars.

"Instead of being rewarded for my hard work and loyalty," she added, "I am left with a lawsuit against my employer and those responsible."[9]

Who does she blame? She leaves no doubt. "Enron executives let us down, the auditors let us down, Wall Street analysts let us down, and the companies lending the money to Enron let us down," Farmer told the *London Guardian*, "but at the end of the day, when the dust settles, who has the greatest pain and greatest losses? We do."[10]

These Enron employees, and thousands more just like them, once felt intoxicated by the company's culture of success that led to a rapid rise in their personal portfolios. Enron seemed like the place to be; didn't the elite in the business world call it home? Yet none of them knew that despair and trouble waited right around the corner.

A STIMULATING PLACE TO BE

After Enron's house of cards began tumbling down, news reports about a diseased company culture started to flood the media. Astonishing stories about rapacious greed, over-the-top arrogance, brutal power plays, and "I want it now" impatience dominated the headlines. And we wondered, *Why would anyone want to work there in the first place?*

In regard to one set of folks, the answer seemed simple enough. For the highly intelligent addicted to a fast pace and lots of money, Enron felt like a stimulating place to be. In fact, for anyone who wanted to be where things were happening, Enron was *the* place.

Young MBA Brian Cruver desperately wanted an offer of employment from Enron. "Highly respected, bitterly admired—if you were craving the fast track, you dreamed of working at Enron," he wrote.[11] Everything moved *fast* at Enron. You could often find bright, young, wealth-creating phenoms traveling on a supersonic Concorde if a corporate plane seemed too full or just too slow.

Yet Enron also attracted the virtuous, the trustworthy, and the straightforward. Thousands of ex-Enron employees can still hold their heads high. Why then did so many of these good, hardworking, and honest people stay at Enron and continue to do their best? Many would tell you they just could not believe that what they saw and knew was happening could kill the company. Most trusted Ken Lay; many still do. While few ever trusted Jeff Skilling, they did think he knew how to make money. Only too late did they discover that he just could not build anything to last.

WHY DID ENRON COLLAPSE?

Enron did not collapse because it failed to accept and even handsomely reward failure at the executive levels—in fact, it regularly handed out bountiful awards.

Enron did not collapse because it neglected to fairly compensate, gift, and entertain its board members—in fact, board members began to count on the company's largesse.

Enron did not collapse because it refused to contribute huge sums to politicians and political causes—in fact, it made large political contributions a habit.

Enron did not collapse because it amassed too few bright, B-school grads—in fact, it had loads of them.

So then, if Enron did not collapse because of any of these things, what *did* happen? Couldn't it find banks to loan it enough money? Couldn't it afford enough expert financial expertise to help construct complicated but legally acceptable ways to manage and fully disclose its debt? Couldn't its board of directors offer some sage advice or ask the right questions or analyze the critical data and reports to fulfill its fiduciary responsibilities?

Of course it could.

Then *what*? Perhaps Enron ran into trouble because it kept too many real assets—that is, things that are actually worth money—too long. In the old days, Enron had assets—pipelines, oil, gas properties, and power plants—worth cash money. The new B-schoolers, however, supported by other fresh-faced B-schoolers from very expensive business consulting firms, had helped the stodgy old asset-based company turn the corner. They taught Enron how to really leverage its assets to amass some meaningful debt and get really creative at Making Money, The New Way.

Skilling and his followers held the old in contempt. Why settle for single-digit rates of growth over decades? Why not liquidate, create new markets, and leave the old businesses in the broadband of their dust? (Cough.)

No. Enron did not collapse due to any of the factors just mentioned. In essence it blew itself to bits by making executive profit its solitary concern. In so doing it became the poster child for a capitalism run amok.

FINDING A NEW MANTRA

When the dust finally settles on this sad chapter of American history, the nation will have to find a new business mantra. To right the wrongs of Enron and protect against similar abuses in the future, it will take more than tougher corporate laws; it will take a change of heart.

As James the brother of Jesus said,

> You know that as soon as the sun rises, pouring down its
> scorching heat, the flower withers. Its petals wilt and, before
> you know it, that beautiful face is a barren stem. Well, that's a
> picture of the 'prosperous life.' At the very moment everyone
> is looking on in admiration, it fades away to nothing.[12]

When affluence and material prosperity become our all-consuming goal, greed takes the wheel and drives the whole speeding convoy over a cliff.

Thankfully, though, our very natural desire for abundance can also call out the best in us: a deep longing to work, create, improve upon, and order our world. Remember, it was God who at the very beginning instructed humankind to subdue the earth and all that is in it.[13] And it is also God who promises that the time will come "for destroying those who destroy the earth."[14]

The catastrophe of Enron shows that it is past time for America to examine the motives behind its unyielding quest for wealth. Our frenzy to accumulate money and power harms not only the poor of America and the rest of the world's underprivileged, but also the very ones who get trapped in a never-ending thirst for more.

As we'll see in the chapters that follow, it does not have to be this way. None of us have to wind up spending our days "drinking white wine and gin" in a neighborhood bar.

Thank God there is so much more to life than that.

CHAPTER 2

An Era of Infectious Greed

On one occasion when Enron Chairman and CEO Ken Lay fielded questions from his employees in the grand ballroom of downtown Houston's Hyatt Regency, some brave, irreverent, or simply dimwitted worker asked Lay why he'd allowed Jeff Skilling's group to cut a hole through a floor in the office to install a spiral staircase.

"Because they're making money," Ken said.

Lay's statement reminded at least one employee, an accountant, of a similar answer several years earlier when concern arose regarding a small group of oil traders raking in millions of dollars: "Leave them alone, they're making money."

By now, of course, we know a little more of the truth. In fact, these oil trading "money makers" had set up separate books and were actually *losing* over $100 million, before taxes. And today we look at the bright young guy at the head of the company, once credited with creating billions of dollars of wealth, and see him spending his days drinking white wine and gin in a neighborhood bar, while an unknown flock of others lose or sell their homes because this failed leader and his business associates lacked not only honor, but common decency.[1]

Look around you. Greed has taken America by storm.

STRIVING FOR MORE . . . AND MORE . . . AND MORE . . .

The September 2002 edition of *Fortune* magazine ran a gutsy article headlined, "The Greedy Bunch."[2] It listed "the 25 companies with the greediest executives," naming the corporate officers and directors who from January 1999 through May 2002 took out the most money via stock sales, even though their company stocks had dropped 75 percent or more from their heydays.

Number 9 on that hit parade hails from Enron. Meet Lou Pai, former division head of several Enron subsidiaries. Perhaps you remember Pai from other news reports. He's the executive who used strippers as a part of business lunches to liven things up a bit.[3]

On the economic side, Pai sold over $994 million worth of Enron stock before the company's collapse, making over *$350 million* in profit. SEC records show that he "cashed out more stock than any Enron executive, more than three times the amount liquidated by Enron Chief Executive Officer Ken Lay."[4] After dumping his stock, Pai bought one of the largest and most historic ranches in the Rocky Mountain West, a seventy-seven-thousand-acre spread on the west slope of Colorado's Sangre de Cristo Mountains, now known as "Mount Pai."

In telling this astonishing story of voracious greed, the normally staid *Fortune* abandoned its usual measured cadences for a decidedly more impassioned approach. "You Bought. They Sold. All over corporate America, top execs were cashing in stock even as their companies were tanking," read the article's subhead. "Who was left holding the bag? You."

And then the magazine got really irritated.

> Over the past few months, the public has been treated to an
> ever-lengthening parade of corporate villains, each seemingly

more rapacious than the last. First there were the Enronites, led by the now disgraced Kenney Lay, Fifth-Amendmenting their way through the halls of Congress. . . . These people and a handful of others are the poster children for the "infectious greed" that Fed chairman Alan Greenspan described recently to Congress. But by now, with the feverish flush of the new economy recognizable as a symptom not of a passion but of an illness, it has also become clear that the mores and practices that characterize this greed suffused the business world far beyond Enron.

Want proof? Then realize that Pai landed only at Number 9 for a reason. Eight other executives grabbed more than he did—some, a lot more. "Executives and directors at a software maker called Ariba raked in $1.24 billion even as its stock was falling from $150 to around $3," barked *Fortune*, adding,

> Peregrine Systems, a deeply troubled software company that is on its third auditor in six months, has announced that it will restate years of revenues, and faces delisting from Nasdaq. Its stock is below 40 cents. But not to worry. Back before anyone realized that its revenues were misstated, chairman John Moores cashed out $646 million, enough to cover the losses of the San Diego Padres, which he also owns, for the next 85 years.

TEETH ON BOTH SIDES

Greed is a snarling monster with a set of razor-sharp teeth on both sides of its head. It devours not only those from whom it takes, but also those who eagerly receive its plunder.

The traders (or traitors?) of Enron should have heeded the New Testament counsel of James, the brother of Jesus. It's almost as if this ancient leader saw the Enron collapse coming thousands of years before it occurred:

> And a final word to you arrogant rich: Take some lessons in lament. You'll need buckets for the tears when the crash comes upon you. Your money is corrupt and your fine clothes stink. Your greedy luxuries are a cancer in your gut, destroying your life from within. You thought you were piling up wealth. What you've piled up is judgment. All the workers you've exploited and cheated cry out for judgment. The groans of the workers you used and abused are a roar in the ears of the Master Avenger. You've looted the earth and lived it up. But all you'll have to show for it is a fatter than usual corpse. In fact, what you've done is condemn and murder perfectly good persons, who stand there and take it.[5]

Left unchecked, this constant striving for more has fatal consequences. Working and creating easily become plundering and pillaging. In no time at all, wolves start masquerading as shepherds, with the public left largely unprotected.

"Watch out!" Jesus warned. "Be on your guard against all kinds of greed; a man's life does not consist in the abundance of his possessions."[6] It may not, but thousands of us still seem eager to give it a try.

BUT CAN IT SATISFY?

Material wealth reigns in the Western world. Money buys power, influence, prestige, health care, companionship, and an untold number of other material "goodies." In the classic movie *Citizen Kane*, Charles Foster Kane, the wealthiest man in the world, builds a veritable castle called Xanadu, fills it with art and statuary from around the globe, and surrounds it with grounds that include "the biggest private zoo since Noah." His every word, his every action, becomes news.

Great wealth can make the entire world your platform—just ask Lance Bass of *NSYNC. This American pop star recently spent several weeks training with Russian cosmonauts in pursuit of his dream to rocket into space at the diminutive cost of $20 million. Lance already owned fast cars, luxurious homes, and took exotic vacations, so he sought the previously unattainable. A flight to the moon? He just might get it.

Because money buys and attracts power, influence, and prestige, then is it possible that multibillionaires such as Donald Trump and Bill Gates have grown satisfied with their level of wealth? Not likely. In fact, if they resemble most Americans, these men feel driven by an insatiable hunger for "stuff." Orson Welles' Charles Foster Kane bought and bought and bought—he filled his castle, then he filled warehouses. He had so many things that he didn't even know what he had. And still he went on, making money, spending money.

Even as our culture encourages and entices people to spend their lives pushing to achieve more, to increase their power, status, and influence, it grinds their faces into the reeking turf of unfulfilled longings and unreachable desire. As we spend our days yearning for more, we grow increasingly dissatisfied with our current state, resent our present situation, and develop a deep discontent for how things really are. Citizen Kane died alone, unhappy, surrounded by the things he had bought and the mansion he had built—the richest man in the world, but also the poorest.

In the end, neither our striving nor the things we buy can save us.

And too late we find truth in the words of a man who at the end of his life regretted his own striving for more:

> I denied myself nothing my eyes desired;
>> I refused my heart no pleasure.
> My heart took delight in all my work,
>> and this was the reward for all my labor.
> Yet when I surveyed all that my hands had done
>> and what I had toiled to achieve,
> everything was meaningless, a chasing after the wind;
>> nothing was gained under the sun.[7]

A GRIM SPIRITUAL REALITY

This continual striving for more reflects something far worse than a mere glitch in the American psyche. In fact, it reveals a grim spiritual reality present in every human heart, a terrible flaw that gives birth to a deep distrust of God.

By assuming that we deserve something better than what we already have, we imply that our Creator must be holding out on us. We find it easy to disbelieve God when he tells us things like, "He who did not spare his own Son, but gave him up for us all—how will he not also, along with him, graciously give us all things?"[8]

Because we do not believe that God truly has our best interests at heart, we take matters into our own hands. We see something we want, we go for it, and oftentimes we get it. And then we congratulate ourselves on our skill and cunning. The author of Deuteronomy spoke of this very danger to his audience in tough words that sound as though he meant them for us today:

Make sure you don't forget GOD, your God, by not keeping his commandments, his rules and regulations that I command you today. Make sure that when you eat and are satisfied, build pleasant houses and settle in, see your herds and flocks flourish and more and more money come in, watch your standard of living going up and up—make sure you don't become so full of yourself and your things that you forget GOD, your God, the God who delivered you from Egyptian slavery; the God who led you through that huge and fearsome wilderness, those desolate, arid badlands crawling with fiery snakes and scorpions; the God who gave you water gushing from hard rock; the God who gave you manna to eat in the wilderness, something your ancestors had never heard of, in order to give you a taste of the hard life, to test you so that you would be prepared to live well in the days ahead of you. If you start thinking to yourselves, "I did all this. And all by myself. I'm rich. It's all mine!"— well, think again. Remember that GOD, your God, gave you the strength to produce all this wealth so as to confirm the covenant that he promised to your ancestors—as it is today.[9]

It's when we forget God and the fact that it is he who gives us the very air we breathe that we land in trouble. And often that trouble can look very different from what many expect.

A PLAGUE OF WEALTH

When most of us think of trouble, we think of hardships and disease and accidents and domestic turmoil. Images of poverty and squalor and wretchedness come to mind. And yet the real trouble we get often wears a very different face.

In ancient times God led the Israelites out of slavery, where their children had been euthanized, the Egyptians had treated them brutally, and they lacked basic religious freedom. God intimidated their captors with terrifying plagues, parted the Red Sea to make possible their escape, and led them by pillars of cloud and fire to a good land he had promised to give them. On their journey to freedom, water burst from the rocks and manna rained daily from the sky.

And how did the people respond to this remarkable provision? They began to complain. "We want meat!" they demanded. "We're sick of this funky bread!"

So God, in his infinite wisdom, gave these ungrateful, murmuring people exactly what they asked for. "I'll give you meat," he said, "and you will eat it. Not for one day, ten days, or twenty—you will eat it until you vomit it out your nostrils."[10]

Trouble . . . in the form of *plenty*? You bet.

It seems that in these days God has done the same for America: "You want wealth? I will give you obscene wealth—and it will lead to your destruction."

Ralph Winter writes,

> The underdeveloped societies suffer from one set of diseases: tuberculosis, malnutrition, pneumonia, parasites, typhoid, cholera, typhus, etc. Affluent America has virtually invented a whole new set of diseases: obesity, arteriosclerosis, heart disease, stroke, lung cancer, venereal disease, cirrhosis of the liver, drug addiction, alcoholism, divorce, battered children, suicide, murder. Take your choice. Labor-saving machines

have turned out to be body-killing devices. Our affluence has
allowed both mobility and isolation of the nuclear family,
and as a result our divorce courts, our prisons and our mental
institutions are flooded. In saving ourselves we have nearly
lost ourselves.[11]

As Winter so disturbingly points out, in many ways our wealth
has become a plague upon us. Yet this plague is more than physical.
Juxtapose for a moment the extravagance of our culture and the opulence of its financial elite with the AIDS crisis in Africa and the
desperate global shortage of food. While a famine of the body ravages
the Third World, a famine of spirit devastates our own.

Dr. Martin Luther King Jr., who often spoke of the interconnectedness of human beings in his struggles for the dignity and rights
of his people, gradually came to realize that the Civil Rights struggle
was only a part of a larger struggle for the peace and dignity of all
people. In his acceptance speech for the Nobel Peace Prize in 1964,
Dr. King closed his remarks with these words: "I have the audacity
to believe that peoples everywhere can have three meals a day for their
bodies, education and culture for their minds, and dignity, equality,
and freedom for their spirits. I believe that what self-centered men
have torn down, other-centered men can build up."[12]

The ultimate lesson of Enron is this: Wealth can never satisfy.
Oh, it can afford some fleeting titillations and for awhile give the
illusion of control, but somehow it always leaves a hole bigger than
the one it tried to fill. As King Solomon, the wisest man (and one of
the richest) who ever lived, said, "whoever loves money never has
money enough; whoever loves wealth is never satisfied with his
income."[13]

THE LOVE OF MONEY

The love of money, which the apostle Paul called "a root of all kinds of evil,"[14] plagues all people, even (and sometimes especially) people of faith. Televangelists want more satellites; pastors and rabbis and imams want bigger houses of worship. Why should businesspeople who profess faith be any different?

In the months before the collapse of Enron, Ken Lay granted an interview to the authors of a book about "Christian CEOs." The book set out to profile leaders who saw their career in business as a divine call. Though many believe Lay shouldn't be blamed for the Enron collapse, editors pulled his contribution from the book. I wonder how many "Executive Officers for Christ" will have scandals surround them?

Of course, such financial scandals existed long before our time. Way back in the first century, the apostle Paul employed pointed rhetoric to warn his friends about corporate excess: "If it's only money these leaders are after, they'll self-destruct in no time. Lust for money brings trouble and nothing but trouble. Going down that path, some lose their footing in the faith completely and live to regret it bitterly ever after."[15]

Some theologians and pastors have justified financial excess as a blessing from God. They see abundance as God's stamp of approval on their chosen lifestyles and like to think of it as a reward for personal righteousness. They think, *If God didn't like what he saw, then why would he gift certain people so richly?* But listen to another perspective:

> A wealth-and-prosperity doctrine is afoot today, shaped by
> the half-truth that says, "We glorify God with our money by
> enjoying thankfully all the things he enables us to buy. Why

should a son of the King live like a pauper?" and so on. The true half of this is that we should give thanks for every good thing God enables us to have. That does glorify him. The false half is the subtle implication that God can be glorified in this way by all kinds of luxurious purchases.

If this were true, Jesus would not have said, "Sell your possessions and give alms" (Luke 12:33). He would not have said, "Do not seek what you are to eat and what you are to drink" (Luke 12:29). John the Baptist would not have said, "He who has two coats, let him share with who has none" (Luke 3:11). The Son of Man would not have walked around with no place to lay his head (Luke 9:58). And Zacchaeus would not have given half his goods to the poor (Luke 19:8).

God is not glorified when we keep for ourselves (no matter how thankfully) what we ought to be using to alleviate the misery of unevangelized, uneducated, unmedicated, and unfed millions. The evidence that many professing Christians have been deceived by this doctrine is how little they give and how much they own. God *has* prospered them. And by an almost irresistible law of consumer culture (baptized by a doctrine of health, wealth, and prosperity) they have bought bigger (and more) houses, newer (and more) cars, fancier (and more) clothes, better (and more) meat, and all manner of trinkets and gadgets and containers and equipment to make life more fun.

The promoters of this 'me first' theology will object: does not the Old Testament promise that God will prosper his people? Indeed! God increases our yield so that by giving we can prove our yield is not our god. God does not prosper a man's business so he can move from a Ford to a Cadillac. God prospers a business so that thousands of unreached peoples can be reached with the gospel. He prospers a business so that twelve percent of the world's population can move a step back from the precipice of starvation.[16]

We might legitimately see the extraordinary wealth of the Western world as an opportunity to give our riches to the starving and dying poor—a kind of test of our generosity. If this is so, we must admit that so far we have failed.

By nature, humankind strives for more than its current lot. Men and women the world over want more than they have, so whenever possible many of them do whatever it takes to get it. Greed remains a powerful motivator—and God knew this from the beginning of his covenant with the Jews. Through the Torah and through the words of the prophets, he urged the creation of a society built on integrity, justice, and truth. These attributes are the only reliable watchdogs against ravenous greed.

THE BEAUTY OF GIVING

The "infectious greed" that Alan Greenspan railed against in Congress cannot be eliminated through rivers of new legislation flowing out of Washington. The only sure remedy is a change of heart, starting with you and me.

Are you willing to rethink the way you use your monetary wealth and rediscover the beauty of giving? The Judeo-Christian tradition offers clear direction about what we willingly offer back to God to use for his greater purposes. The Hebrew Scriptures talk a great deal about giving a tithe (10 percent of income), while the New Testament opens the floodgates and encourages us toward a boundary-busting generosity. So the apostle Paul can say, "You will be made rich in every way so that you can be generous on every occasion."[17]

The British writer C. S. Lewis thought deeply on this topic and believed that the best way to break money's power over us is to give it away; yet he shrank from suggesting a rigid formula for giving. "I do not believe one can settle how much we ought to give," he wrote.

> I am afraid the only safe rule is to give more than we can spare. In other words, if our expenditure on comforts, luxuries, amusements, etc., is up to the standard common among those with the same income as our own, we are probably giving away too little. If our charities do not at all pinch or hamper us, I should say they are too small. There ought to be things we should like to do and cannot do because our charitable expenditure excludes them.[18]

What would happen in our world if businesspeople began acting on Lewis's simple suggestion? What would happen in our nation if both executives and laborers began practicing a kind of generosity that "pinched"? What would happen in your own neighborhood if *you* gave more than you could spare?

Why not stop thinking about it and instead actually give it a try?

CHAPTER 3

Kenneth Lay: Crooked, Clueless, or Consumed by a Fast-Paced Culture?

Perhaps it should surprise no one that Ken Lay, former chairman of the board and CEO of energy-trading giant Enron, has kept quiet regarding the demoralizing collapse of his Fortune 500 enterprise. What, after all, could he say?

Either he colluded with top executives in the disastrous deals that tore Enron apart, or he sat by, uncomprehending, during top-level discussions of the company's off-book partnerships and suspicious accounting practices. Or was the company just too large and the amount of managerial restraint beyond what he could exert? Crooked or clueless or consumed by fast-paced culture — not much of a choice, is it?

And given the magnitude of Enron's collapse — company stock soared to $90 a share only a year before Enron's "creative accounting" came to the public's attention, then fell to twenty-six cents a share in November 2001, and finally was dropped altogether from the New York Stock Exchange in January 2002 — I doubt I'd have much to say, either. Except, possibly, "I'm sorry."

A MODEL CEO

Lay's career in energy began in 1965 when he joined what is now ExxonMobil as a corporate economist in Houston, Texas. He was twenty-three years old.

Lay became CEO of Houston Natural Gas in 1984 after two decades of work in the energy industry all across the United States. After taking the position, Lay quickly engineered the acquisitions of Transwestern Pipeline and Florida Gas. The next year, before the company could digest these buyouts, he and his team found themselves being pulled into a potential merger with the much larger Omaha-based pipeline company, Internorth. Lay quickly outmaneuvered his counterpart at Internorth and its board of directors and became CEO of the combined company, which in February 1986 changed its name to the now-infamous Enron.

Lay presided over Enron's metamorphosis from old-market energy company to new-market trading company, and many considered the turn nothing short of miraculous. Executives and pundits held up Lay as a model CEO.

Lay relinquished his role as CEO in February 2001 — in order to devote his attention to politics, some claimed, where he and Enron had always heavily invested — in favor of his protégé, Jeffrey Skilling. Lay returned as CEO in August 2001 only after Skilling unexpectedly resigned for "personal reasons."

Lay remained chairman of Enron's board for almost all of this tumultuous sixteen-year period until he was asked to resign on January 23, 2002, just as the United States Senate Commerce Committee issued a subpoena requesting his testimony regarding a lawsuit against Enron. Lay resigned altogether from the board in February 2002.

A HATED EVANGELIST?

Lay, now considered by some to be the most hated man in America, first earned a reputation as an evangelist in the energy business, converting tens of thousands to follow his lead in the ultraprofitable energy-trading industry that he created.

But eventually the messiah became a serpent in the minds of countless erstwhile disciples. In scores of interviews with ex-Enroners, one hears statements like these:

- "I put my faith in Enron."
- "I believed in Ken Lay."
- "Everything he touched turned to gold."
- "I had faith in our CEO."

Here we see a sad thing: misplaced faith and off-balance devotion. Today men and women all over the country are reaping the consequences of putting their faith in temporary things that ultimately go sour. For as it is written—and as many of these men and women have discovered firsthand—these things shall pass away.[1]

POINTING FINGERS

Many quickly pointed the finger at Lay, demanding that he justify his actions and the sordid behavior of his failed company. Investors lost billions and felt they had a right to know what went wrong.

Consider Charles Prestwood, a sixty-three-year-old retired plant operations worker who spent thirty-three years working the pipelines in the oil and gas industry, the last fifteen with Enron. At peak, his 13,500 shares were worth about $1.3 million. He lost 99 percent of his savings when Enron collapsed.

"I lost everything I had,"[2] Prestwood laments. "There ain't no such thing as a dream anymore. I hadn't planned much for the retirement. Wanted to go fishing, hunting. I was gonna travel a little."[3]

Prestwood survives on a pension from a previous employer—less than $550 a month after health insurance and income tax—and a Social Security check of less than $1,300. "I'm not gonna be able to last long like that," he confesses.

> I got some land that I wanted to give to my kids. That land was given to me by my mother. My mother died when I was born. I can go in the cemetery and look upon her tombstone, that's the day I was born, September the 15th, 1938. That land was the only thing other than the family Bible that she left me. My daddy and her, they had an agreement: If something happened to her and her baby lived, she wanted her portion of the property to go to the baby, and my daddy right there said, "If something happens to you, I'll give the baby my part too." And my daddy did, in November of 1938; he deeded that eight acres. I've got to sell that land now. That'll take care of a few more of them house notes.[4]

Today he lives on a three-acre farm in Conroe, Texas, sixty miles north of Houston; he owns two horses and a feed barn. "I'm just a hardworking country boy," he says, continuing,

> When I graduated from high school in May of 1957, I never missed a payday until I retired on October the 1st of 2000. Worked construction for a while, and welding, then I went to work for Houston Natural Gas Systems in March of 1967, started in maintenance, at $2.78 an hour, sweeping the side-

walks, emptying the trash cans, mopping the floors. I was there when Internorth and Houston Natural merged in 1985 and Enron was born. I was with 'em all the way, from the very beginning, 33 and [a] half years. We had a goal: We wanted to be the No. 1 gas supplier. My job on the pipeline was keeping the gas flowing to our customers. I worked all my life devoted to it. That's what's so hurting—so hurting down deep in your heart: When you work a whole lifetime and help build something, you feel like you had a part in building Enron . . . and then to see it tore down right in front of your eyes. [5]

Faithful workers like Prestwood who eagerly invested in the Houston-based firm suffered great loss when Wall Street dropped Enron's stock from trading on the New York Stock Exchange. The fall of this supposedly great corporation also dealt a huge blow to the nation's economy while simultaneously wreaking havoc on thousands of families nationwide. A current study indicates that the combined failures of Enron and WorldCom will ultimately cost the United States economy $37 to $42 *billion* in reduced gross domestic product. [6]

A MAJOR DISCONNECT

It doesn't take a master theologian to notice the obvious disconnect between the massive harm inflicted on others for selfish gain and the serve-others-first message of Christ.

Lay has long professed to be a Bible-believing follower of Christ, a Christian businessman holding to Christian values and ethics—and in many eyes that makes the spectacular failure of his company all the more egregious. In an interview with *The Door* magazine in 2001, for example, Lay assured Robert Darden, "My employees know that I take basic religious principles very seriously" and "It's widely known that I have a very strong Christian background and Christian faith."[7]

But can anyone live a genuine faith without that faith guiding and coloring everything one does, including one's activities in the business world? The Bible tells us that faith without works is dead.[8] So what about integrity? What about commandments such as "Thou shalt not steal," and "Thou shalt not bear false witness"? The list goes on.

Lay, who was inducted into the Texas Business Hall of Fame in 1997,[9] says,

> Throughout my life, things have fallen into place that turned out to be the right thing to do at the time. Looking back, this door opened, then this door opened, and maybe then that door closed. I always picked the thing that seemed to be the most interesting, the most fun. But looking back, 30 or 40 years later in some cases, those were the things that just really fit together perfectly for the career I've had. I am convinced that God was—and is—guiding all the way. There is something fascinating about business that has always fascinated me. I think, in my case, I've been able to make a bigger and more positive impact through business than I could have in any other profession, including the ministry. I've been able to impact more lives, more communities, and more causes than I could have otherwise.[10]

Well, Lay certainly has made an impact—but I have a serious problem with the idea that God guided Ken Lay to create the cynical, soul-eating culture of Enron, and to either protect or avoid knowing how the top people under his employ appear to have been looting the company's coffers.

MORE THAN GENEROSITY NEEDED

It's commendable that Ken Lay has given generously to worthy causes—and he has: He has funded everything from literacy projects to church-starting efforts. A Christian whose net worth can be measured in hundreds of millions of dollars has a responsibility—a sacred duty, even—to be generous. But I can't help but recall that Jesus commended not the tycoons who donated large sums to the temple treasury, but rather the poor widow who gave literally her last two cents. "I tell you the truth," Jesus told his disciples, "this poor widow has put more into the treasury than all the others. They all gave out of their wealth; but she, out of her poverty, put in everything—all she had to live on."[11]

As much as Lay's gifts may have amounted to, he certainly didn't impoverish himself through his largesse (and no, that's not a requirement). Today the Lays still own eleven homes in Houston. One of them, their primary residence, covers seventeen-thousand square feet and takes up an entire floor in a prestigious high rise in Houston. Estimated cost of that one home? Around $6 million.

A REFUSAL TO TAKE RESPONSIBILITY

What enrages many about the perceived gap between Lay's professed beliefs and his record at Enron is not the monetary success; bright, innovative, hardworking Christians almost can't help (and should not be ashamed of) making money. What makes them furious is his apparent refusal to take even partial responsibility for what happened.

After Sherron Watkins and others bluntly warned him that accounting disasters riddled the firm and could ruin Enron, it appears Lay took no decisive action. And he somehow failed to give his employees an accurate portrait of the company's health. In August 2001, just after Skilling's departure and after Lay had received Sherron Watkins' memo on the state of the company, *Business Week* asked the chairman, "There has been some concern among investors that perhaps there is more to [Skilling's] resignation than meets the eye, perhaps accounting or other issues that have yet to come to light. Is there anything more?" Lay replied, "There are no accounting issues, no trading issues, no reserve issues, no previously unknown problem issues. The company is probably in the strongest and best shape that it has ever been in. There are no surprises. . . . And, if there were any serious problems, they would be in there. If there's anything material and we're not reporting it, we'd be breaking the law. We don't break the law."[12]

In the turbulent wake of Skilling's departure, and even after the initial reports of Enron's woeful accounting, Lay led pep rallies and sent company-wide memos to assure employees that all was well. He even encouraged them to buy more Enron stock. On October 23, 2001, 1600 employees listened as Lay apologized for the loss in value of Enron stock. Yet he remained upbeat. "We're going to get it back," he declared, and then announced that bonuses would still be paid if Enron met its targets. Those in attendance noted that he seemed sincere. Whether that was because he was telling the truth, believed he was telling the truth, or was simply spouting the most optimistic answer in the face of doom, they could not tell.[13] And in multiple off-the-record conversations with Lay, neither can I.

So the verdict is still out: crooked, clueless, or consumed by a fast-paced culture? We won't know until Ken Lay finally goes "on the record," something he has strictly avoided up to the present.

CHAPTER 4

The Disaster of Dualism

Close to 1:00 A.M. on what had become yet another late work night, Kim, a disgusted human resources veteran at Enron, quit her job. A coworker argued with her, citing some first-rate financial advice: "Bonuses are only a few weeks off. Wait until you get paid what you've earned, and then resign."

But Kim left hastily, forfeiting thousands of dollars. Why? She could no longer tolerate her involvement with one of Enron's less-publicized outrages, the annual Performance Review program.[1]

Kim's superiors considered her a valuable asset and did everything they could to keep her. They offered her a large raise, even a bonus. But not even the entire coffers of Enron contained enough money to make Kim change her mind.

You might be wondering at this point: *What could have left such a sour taste in Kim's mouth that she would willingly give up so much money? What was wrong with her?* After all, others seemed to have no problem with the "rank-and-yank" system, introduced and championed by Jeff Skilling, the genius who was "making money." At the very least, others managed to hold their tongues and tolerate a system that lacked any consideration for what was just and fair.

But not Kim.

Actually, it's hard to see how *anyone* with a fundamental gut feeling of right and wrong could continue to participate in such an unfair and degrading system as the Performance Review program at Enron. The Performance Review Committees (PRCs) divided workers into rating groups, from best to worst; the bottom rankings meant potentially lower compensation, reassignment, or termination. In theory, perhaps, it was a workable (if heartless) system. But in practice it became a barrel of Faustian bargains that compromised everyone involved.

When "rank-and-yank" time came, committees discussed the performance of departmental employees with the division manager, who was responsible to represent the employees under his or her supervision. As the PRC meetings dragged along and the managers had to stay within "preferred" distribution percentages, some resorted to bartering. One manager might be willing to downgrade an employee or two in exchange for a higher slot freed up by another manager. As tension mounted, managers raised their voices and descended to their worst behavior. The loudest and most temperamental sometimes overcame those with sounder arguments who yet refused to get down in the gutter.

Kim's friend described these meetings as the embodiment of evil, a living hell. She could not bear the nonchalant nature of the game. These were people's lives the managers were trading back and forth, not baseball cards or parking spaces.

The operation of the Performance Review Committees led to a growing heap of lies and untruths. Managers were taught to misinform employees by stating that performance distribution percentages were "preferred," but not rigid or mandatory. Enron executives required their managers to tell workers, "Your rating is relative to the performance of your peers across the company." After all, what would happen to employee morale if workers discovered they could have the most productive year of their careers, but only a small minority would receive the golden apple?

Moreover, if managers were forced to downgrade an employee to meet the ranking distributions (called "slamming"), they couldn't tell that employee what had happened. How would it feel to be told you were being fired because you had been "traded" to free up certain tiers for other employees?

Kim left Enron to get away from the evil she witnessed. She could not bear to see the careers of valuable employees get bartered into oblivion—and she was not the only one so distressed.

Consider the employee hired to train managers to say that they could not attribute an employee's low performance rating to the "preferred" percentages. Unwilling to lie, she skirted the issue in her first small meeting. At the second meeting a manager noted that she avoided the issue, and so informed her boss. Finally, in the next training session, the trainer felt so disturbed by the deceit that she broke out in hives and resigned.

And so Enron's efforts to compartmentalize the morality of its workers claimed yet another victim.

ISOLATED BELIEFS

A select group of Enron executives embraced a philosophy so far from traditional ethics that they ended up adopting a lifestyle completely contrary to their company's stated beliefs on integrity. By their actions, they scorned what they publicly said they believed.

In fact, the integrity that Enron so skillfully advocated in its public relations brochures turned out to be as fictional as the corporation's publicly proclaimed profits. On the whole, Enron not only rejected the practice of integrity, it did not seem to recognize the tiniest part of its existence. How can this be?

In his book *The Divine Conspiracy*, Dallas Willard writes, "We must face the fact that human beings can honestly profess to believe what they do not believe. They may do this for so long that even they no longer know that they do not believe what they profess. But their actions will, of course, be in terms of what they actually believe."[2]

We humans—and not just former executives at Enron—have a frightening ability to declare our belief in one thing while simultaneously acting in a manner 180 degrees in opposition to it. Some have used the term "isolated beliefs" to describe this phenomenon. We isolate our beliefs from our actions in such a way that either we do not see or do not care that the two violently clash with one another.

This clash can undercut the common assumption that man is basically good, and it certainly shows how a warped kind of capitalism that feeds on greed can eventually lead to the collapse of personal ethics. *Laissez-faire* capitalism is all about the survival of the fittest, and the survival of the fittest means that someone "less fit" must suffer for our gain. The system is flawed; it feeds on the vile and selfish side of man—and this is no new idea.

Economist Adam Smith wrote in *The Wealth of Nations* (published, significantly, in the year 1776) that corporations have the greatest tendency toward evil—as opposed to partnerships or fully owned companies—because corporations separate ownership from control. Instead of the owners running the business, managers run it for owner-stockholders. Nineteenth-century rubber baron William Henry Vanderbilt once famously proclaimed, "The public be damned! I'm working for my stockholders."

Such a mentality drives every corporate decision that causes hardship to local economies; every decision to outsource labor to less-regulated, less-protected workers; every refusal to comply with the "voluntary" Bush administration pollution standards. The public be damned! To pay attention to such things might deflate the price of the stock or reduce the stream of profits.

The Enron case and others scattered around it like a shotgun pattern show what happens when greedy managers make self-enrichment their solitary goal. At Enron and WorldCom and many other recent busts, top executives abused their trust to rape the companies under their care. Only integrity and honesty can hold the capitalistic system in check. When they disappear, everything is up for grabs.

Enron—although an extreme case—is, of course, hardly the only company with a hollow set of values. A former Enron executive said, "Most values statements are bland, toothless, or just plain dishonest. And far from being harmless, as some executives assume, they're often highly destructive. Empty values statements create cynical and dispirited employees, alienate customers, and undermine management credibility."[3]

While we cannot know whether the Enron executives or public relations gurus who developed their company's values statements ever actually believed what they wrote—perhaps they crafted them merely as a means to gain the trust of clients, without the slightest intention of abiding by them—I'd be willing to guess that, at least at the beginning, many of these leaders felt warm toward the ideals of respect, communication, excellence, and integrity. They honestly wanted to be and be known as individuals who embodied four such noble traits.

And yet, the company ended up violating every one, thus demolishing the hopes and futures of countless men and women who trusted Enron to keep its word. How did this happen?

Lay the blame at the door of dualism.

DUALISM THROUGH CHRISTIAN HISTORY

For much of its history, a large section of Western culture—and, by extension, Western Christianity—has affirmed a belief system marked by a dualist separation between God and world, sacred and secular, heart and mind, soul and body.

Scripture admonishes us to be in the world but not of it,[4] and Christians have often read this to mean that we are purely spiritual beings rather than creatures of both body and spirit. Certainly, Western Christianity since the days of Paul has followed this separation to the letter of the law.

Noteworthy elements of the Christian church have long encouraged an ascetic lifestyle that viewed the things of the world as evil, and the non-corporeal world—consisting of the things of the mind and spirit—as the only universe worth inhabiting.

The early gnostics, for example, sought the spiritual and avoided the physical.

Saint Augustine, in his influential work *The City of God* (written A.D. 413-426), employed the thoughts of Plato on the distinctness of spirit and matter to describe two dissimilar cities, the kingdom of God and the kingdoms of the world.

The Franciscan, Benedictine, and other monastic traditions honored cloistered lives of celibacy and poverty as the most pious of all and painted people of commerce as pawns of Satan. Some monks even resorted to castration (without anesthetic, mind you) to prove their disdain for the flesh and their love of the spirit.

Finally, the French philosopher René Descartes (1596-1650) cemented the Western acceptance of a mind/body dualism with his assertion that the physical realm consisted of things that could be quantified, located in time and space. We still refer to this separation between the worlds of spirit and matter as a "Cartesian dualism"; and most major Western philosophers accepted it until well into the twentieth century.

CHRISTIAN DUALISM TODAY

Such an erroneous dualism still exists in many forms, whether by emphasizing that the life of the spirit and the life of the flesh oppose one another, or more piously, by playing on the idea that by giving up the pleasures of this world we will gain treasure in heaven.

This helps to explain why, all across contemporary America, the same families that fill the pews of local churches each week (representing the model suburban/Christian lifestyle) often live secret lives. Dad is addicted to Internet porn while Mom keeps her teenage figure by purging after big and small meals alike. The children have learned that anything can be bought, even an A in senior English. Everyone believes that faith is great for Sunday mornings—but it gets thrown out before the family sits down for Sunday dinner, and completely spoils by the time the family leaves for work and school on Monday.

Stuff is stuff and spirit is spirit, says this wrongheaded dualism, and never the twain shall meet.

Sex, for example, has become the lightning rod of self-righteous dualists. Because the physical world has no commerce with the spiritual, sex—the most concrete representation of the physical in the minds of many Christians—must be a thing of the Devil. Forget that God created man and woman to enjoy marital sexual pleasure and that this most Holy Lord advertises the blessings of erotic pleasure in Scripture, most notably in the explicit love poetry of King Solomon. The church largely ignores this honest scriptural portrayal of the holy beauty of sex out of fear over dealing with it in an open forum.

In regard to this most obvious manifestation of the dualistic disconnection between the worlds of body and spirit, we might heed the words of the thirteenth-century Jewish commentator Moses Maimonides, who wrote,

> We who are the descendants of those who received the sacred
> Torah believe that God, blessed be He, created everything as
> His wisdom dictated, and He created nothing containing
> obscenity or ugliness. For if we were to say that intercourse is
> obscene, it would follow that the sexual organs are
> obscene. . . . And how could God, blessed be He, create something containing a blemish or obscenity, or a defect? . . . He
> created man and woman, fashioning all their organs and setting
> them in their proper function with nothing obscene in them.[5]

If sex—that most frightening bugaboo of our physical selves—is a divine creation and a divinely sanctioned part of human life, then it seems apparent that *nothing* in the realm of tangible human conduct should be considered separate from our spiritual belief and practice.

Ironically, it seems that some sexually repressed and overly conservative Christians often drown their pent-up frustrations in food—and lots of it. Warnings against gluttony seem to have disappeared from the Scriptures, or at least from the sermons of some portly pulpiteers of American Christendom. And that, even as eating disorders plague a huge percentage of Americans!

For too many of us, the Christian faith appears distinct and even distant from the rest of our lives. Should it surprise us, then, that many twenty-first-century Christians go to great pains to separate their faith from the way they live, do business, and make important decisions?

Our own long adherence to dualism has brought us to this place:

while in the 1970s President Jimmy Carter could admit to having committed adultery in his heart, in the 1990s Bill Clinton could say, in effect, "I have not had sexual relations with that woman—and even if I have, what difference does it make?" The latter president thus provided a stunning example of an influential American—a professing Christian, even—who claimed a complete separation between his personal and professional lives.

Did issues of character and morality have nothing to do with the job of president? Certainly they did. What a person does in private speaks to the whole of his or her life. So if a man will lie to his wife and family, how can we entrust him with the leadership of a nation?

But forget about hot-button presidential politics for a moment. What does it say about contemporary American Christianity when a professing Christian such as Enron CEO Kenneth Lay speaks with eloquence about his faith, even while he is paid tens of millions of dollars to run a company which not only violates the letter of the law, but its spirit as well? What does it say when his company seemingly degrades its employees, and cheats American taxpayers and businesses? It says this: that in our culture, many Christians have separated their worlds so completely that we have come to the verge of economic, ecological, and moral disaster.

Isn't it long past time that we integrated life and faith?

INVITING GOD INTO ALL OF LIFE

Faith does not have to separate itself from life in the everyday world. To demonstrate that fact, both Judaism and Islam honor submission to God and integrate him into daily life.

Judaism reveres those who walk with God in every aspect of their daily lives, following not just the letter of the Torah, but the spirit of it as well. Islam honors the example of Mohammed, who moved his family into the courtyard of a mosque to dramatically illustrate that in submitting to God, there can be no distinction between the place of worship and everyday life.

We American Christians desperately need a new sense of honesty, of integration, of the beauty that can come when faith permeates every aspect of our existence. Archbishop Desmond Tutu of South Africa admonishes us not to segregate our faith, arguing that, "Our God does not permit us to dwell in a kind of spiritual ghetto, insulated from real life out there. Jesus used to go out and be alone with God in deep prayerful meditation, but he did not remain there."[6]

We must rethink any tendency to divide our lives between "worship" and "everyday living." The stakes are simply too high. The apostle Paul recognized the absurdity of misplaced loyalties that creates a culture filled with "trinket gods; magic-show religion; paranoid loneliness; cutthroat competition; all-consuming-yet-never-satisfied wants; a brutal temper; an impotence to love or be loved; divided homes and divided lives; small-minded and lopsided pursuits."[7] This sounds like our America—but this is not how God wants us to live. God calls for us to live lives both wholly authentic and thoroughly engaged.

SPINOZA'S OPPOSITION TO DUALISM

A living, breathing faith cannot be compartmentalized and subjugated to a narrow slice of life. To do so courts disaster; moreover, it offends God's nature—and our own.

The Jewish philosopher Benedict Spinoza, one of René Descartes' few contemporary critics, opposed the idea of dualism (with all his heart and mind). His conclusions stir us still today.

If God is infinite, Spinoza argued, he cannot have boundaries. Therefore, God is not outside the world, nor inside the world; God *encompasses* the world. And human beings "have the same dual character in one being: we are our physical bodies, but we are also our souls, and these are not two different people, they are one and the same person: it is as if, as an ancient Jewish teaching had it, the body is the soul in outward form."[8]

Spinoza's conclusions find resonance in the Christian faith through the doctrine of the Incarnation: God took on flesh and dwelt among us. Jesus came into the world as a whole, integrated person. He engaged all of life as a physical and spiritual being. He did not dwell only in temples among the religious; instead, he cared for all people, including the fraudulent tax collectors, the money-loving politicians, and the down-and-out prostitutes. He did not adopt the ungodly manners and practices of those he traveled among, but consistently proclaimed his uncompromising teachings in both the temple and among the prostitutes (and those who frequented them).

Today, Christ continues to call all of us to a holistic life where faith, family, and commerce intersect. Integrity, where our "yes means yes and our no means no," makes church, business, community, and relationships *work*.

If we do not let our faith inform our daily actions, then perhaps we should no longer claim our faith. Too harsh a conclusion, you say? Maybe so — but I didn't come up with it. Listen to the apostle Paul: "They say they know God, but their actions speak louder than their words. They're real creeps, disobedient good-for-nothings."[9] And it was Paul who publicly declared, "I preached that they should repent and turn to God and *prove their repentance by their deeds*."[10]

Desmond Tutu, an advocate of a Christian movement that looks to the life of Christ to argue for the importance of action in this world as well as the next, has long argued that there must be no separation between our worlds: "Christian faith believes that God uses ordinary material things as vehicles for God's spiritual grace. . . . Our faith is incarnational through and through."[11]

And so it is, although we do not always act it out.

TAKING AN ANCIENT CUE

When I asked a long-time friend and coworker of Ken Lay's about Ken's faith, he replied unwaveringly, "When it comes to faith, Ken's a schizophrenic." Take heed, lest we share the same indictment. At Enron, many workers found their Monday selves in desperate conflict with the selves they had taken to church only a day before. In fact, the culture at Enron encouraged many employees to leave their moral compasses at the front security desk and embrace "the Enron way."

Some did this without thinking, some did it and couldn't sleep at night, and some chose to maintain their convictions—and paid a hefty price for them.

We have to ask ourselves, "Does it have to be so difficult?" Not really. Perhaps we could take a cue from the business practices of the ancient Hebrews:

> In the olden times in Israel, this is how they handled official
> business regarding matters of property and inheritance: a
> man would take off his shoe and give it to the other person.
> This was the same as an official seal or personal signature.[12]

Don't focus on the shoe in this example, but on the unsophisticated integrity that ruled the transaction. In our culture, where politicians lie as a matter of policy, where perjury has become commonplace, where false promises from greedy televangelists screech out from the channels between QVC and CNN, and where everyone might be a potential con artist, we must stand against the cultural flow and determine to become a people worthy of trust. This can occur only when we people of faith remain the same in the marketplace as in our prayer-closets, when the faith we claim animates all our dealings.

"Work from the heart for your real Master, for God," writes the apostle Paul,

> confident that you'll get paid in full when you come into
> your inheritance. Keep in mind always that the ultimate
> Master you're serving is Christ. The sullen servant who does
> shoddy work will be held responsible. Being Christian
> doesn't cover up bad work.[13]

God did not leave the element of human commerce out of his thoughts, as some would have us believe. He has plenty to say in the Bible about work and business. The book of Leviticus spells out many laws of just business practices. The prophet Amos condemned the sort of rapaciousness exemplified by shady deal-making Enron executives and traders, as well as the exploitation of workers and the poor. And the prophet Micah screams out in despair in the midst of an ancient ethical and moral crisis:

> I'm overwhelmed with sorrow!
> Sunk in a swamp of despair!

I'm like someone who goes to the garden
>to pick cabbages and carrots and corn
And returns empty-handed,
>finds nothing for soup or sandwich or salad.
There's not a decent person in sight.
>Right-living humans are extinct.
They're all out for one another's blood,
>animals preying on each other.
They've all become experts in evil.
>Corrupt leaders demand bribes.
The powerful rich
>make sure they get what they want.
The best and brightest are thistles.
>The top of the line is crabgrass.
But no longer: It's exam time.
>Look at them slinking away in disgrace!
Don't trust your neighbor,
>don't confide in your friend.
Watch your words,
>even with your spouse.
Neighborhoods and families are falling to pieces.
>The closer they are — sons, daughters, in-laws —
The worse they can be.
>Your own family is the enemy.
But me, I'm not giving up.
>I'm sticking around to see what GOD will do.
I'm waiting for God to make things right.
>I'm counting on God to listen to me.[14]

Until we heed the counsel of the Creator, corporate culture will continue to embody the vilest forms of selfishness and greed.

So is there no hope on the horizon? Indeed there is. But we will find it not in Congress, not in the courtroom, and not on the trading floors of Wall Street. We will find authentic and potent hope when, as a people, we seek to honor the Creator and all of his creation by living integrated lives.

"It is part of God's mission and purpose for his world," Archbishop Tutu wrote, "to bring about wholeness, justice, good health, righteousness, peace, harmony and reconciliation. . . . And we are his agents to work with him as his partners to bring to pass all that God wants for his universe."[15]

May it be so.

CHAPTER 5

Jeff Skilling: Unbreakable

Just over a year ago, had you been hunting for a corporate hero, your search probably would have led directly to Jeff Skilling.

In April 2001, *Worth* magazine named him number 2 of the fifty top chief executive officers in the nation (behind Microsoft CEO Steve Ballmer) — after less than three months in the position.[1] Those "in the know" widely esteemed Skilling as a management genius and innovative business guru. In fact, he had shined as a leader his entire life, from leading his friends in miscellaneous childhood adventures to spearheading creativity in the adult business world.

Tom Peters, a best-selling management expert who had worked with Skilling at McKinsey & Co., the influential consulting firm, claimed that Skilling "could out-argue God."[2] At Enron, "Skilling was [the company's] chief visionary, head cheerleader, and internal compass," said *BusinessWeek*.[3] "He created and embodied the in-your-face Enron culture, where risk-taking, deal making, and 'thinking outside the box' received rich rewards, while controls appeared loose at best."[4] "Enron was presented externally as a flat organization, but there was never any question who was in charge," says a former Enron trader. "It was Jeff."[5]

Today, no one is calling Jeffrey Skilling a corporate hero. Brilliant? Yes. Clever? Certainly. But a hero? No.

A TALENTED STRATEGIST

Skilling, 48, grew up in New Jersey and Illinois as the son of a successful valve company manager. He studied engineering at Southern Methodist University in Dallas on a full scholarship, and there fell in love with business.

After graduation from SMU, he accepted a job in operations at First City National Bank in Houston and later moved into asset-liability management. The bank folded while Skilling studied for his MBA at Harvard Business School.

Skilling began working with Enron in 1986 as a consultant from McKinsey & Co. James W. Crownover, who hired Skilling at McKinsey's Houston office, remembered him simply as "outstanding in every respect" and "one of the most talented people we ever had."[6] Skilling quickly won the confidence of Enron's founder and then-CEO, Ken Lay, with his innovative ideas about trading natural gas.

Skilling left McKinsey & Co. in 1990 when Lay offered him a full-time position at Enron as head of the company's trading business. Lay once said of Skilling, "I don't think he has a non-strategic bone in his body."[7] Skilling and Lay shared a vision for a greater company. They wanted to transform Enron into a global energy-trading dynasty.

In 1996, Lay made Skilling company president and chief operating officer, and in February 2001 Skilling was named CEO, after Lay stepped down. Everyone considered Jeffrey Skilling the man who would lead Enron into a long and profitable future. Yet he held the position for only six months, resigning unexpectedly in August for "personal reasons," claiming that he wanted to spend more time with family. His surprise resignation from his self-declared "dream job" became the first real indicator of major problems.

Even though Skilling left Enron before the company's collapse, most insiders place the primary blame for the debacle at his doorstep. Even with former CEO Ken Lay returning to the helm, it seemed clear that serious trouble bubbled beneath the surface. Could it be that the very things that made Skilling "successful" also led to his company's demise?

A WORKAHOLIC WHO DEMANDED LOYALTY

While at Enron, Skilling developed an infamous reputation as a workaholic who rarely left the office. Many report that "if Jeff was in the office, [employees] should also be in the office."

Employees quickly learned that to last at Enron one had to prove one's devotion by imitating Jeff's work ethic. Those who chose instead to adopt a normal work schedule in order to be home with their young children either lost their jobs or got continually passed over for promotions.

It was Skilling who brought the infamous employee Performance Review system to Enron, which came to be called "rank and yank" due to its rigid application of preferred performance distribution percentages. Those with strong performance reviews received quick promotions; the bottom fifth got demoted, passed-over, or fired. Skilling and other proponents of the system thought this style of ruthless management kept people on their feet, highly motivated, and always looking over their shoulder.

It appears Skilling demanded unquestioned loyalty, not because of his leadership gifts or integrity, but because his employees received fat paychecks. At least one executive remembers catching the brunt of Skilling's anger for asking too many questions. On one occasion he saw his budget forecasts thrown back in his face, along with the message that if he continued on that path, Jeff would see to it that his career died a slow and painful death.

THE FALL OF PRIDE

In his heyday, Skilling boasted in several interviews that Enron's stock—which hit a high of $90 in August 2000—could easily hit $126 by the end of 2001. Instead, the New York Stock Exchange dropped the company from trading in January 2002.

Investigators in Congress now wonder just how the brilliant and intimidating Skilling ran his company—and whether he orchestrated the accounting scandal that brought down the nation's biggest energy trader. At the time of this writing, he has refused to cooperate with federal investigators or the Senate hearings. "I wasn't there," he customarily replies.

Sources say that Skilling, the leading architect of Enron's trading strategy who "gained a reputation for being tough, confident and full of swagger,"[8] today spends his days at a local bar near his nine-thousand-square-foot Mediterranean mansion in Houston, drinking wine and lamenting the collapse of "The World's Coolest Company."[9]

The author of Proverbs, as though reading the *New York Times* or the *Wall Street Journal* during this past year, speaks truth that echoes through the centuries: "First pride, then the crash—the bigger the ego, the harder the fall."[10] Skilling rose to the top like a shooting star (pride) then fell to the ground like a flaming meteorite (the crash). "Pride lands you flat on your face," says Proverbs.[11]

Wisdom throughout the ages offers all of us potent warnings about the eventual destruction of the arrogant. God promises, "I'll break your strong pride: I'll make the skies above you like a sheet of tin and the ground under you like cast iron."[12]

With that warning in mind, we must all be careful not to gloat over the fall of this brilliant business mind. Instead, let us learn from the downfall of Jeffrey Skilling and examine our own motivations and any longings to massage our own egos. And don't forget, we're all scheduled for our own final performance review:

> For we must all appear before the judgment seat of Christ,
> that each one may receive what is due him for the things
> done while in the body, whether good or bad.[13]

CHAPTER 6

Boast Only in the "E"

"If you let your head get too big, it'll break your neck."[1]

Elvis Presley

Arrogant. That's the most frequently used word to describe Enron.

Former Enron employees who once haughtily strode the streets of Houston's downtown with heads held high now craft new résumés in shame, seeking creative ways to avoid mentioning having worked for the once "Most Innovative Company in America." Things certainly have changed. One aphorism from the first century puts it this way: "There is but a step between a proud man's glory and his disgrace."[2]

THE FUEL OF DECLINE

One cannot describe the fallen shooting star of an epic Fortune 500 corporation without exposing the conceit and self-importance that fueled the company's rapid ascent and painful decline.

Most Enron employees enjoyed being part of a company so widely known and regarded as a "winner." They reveled in the envy of friends, relatives, and new acquaintances who did not work for a company so lofty in the economy of the cool.

Yet "cool" had a way of turning into "arctic." Investigators and observers and even former Enron directors may never understand all of what happened at the fallen corporation although directors must know by now that they made many mistakes and blunders (even if top officials misled them).

When directors do not understand or cannot grasp the business activities of the corporations for which they have fiduciary responsibility (and a whole lot of expensive liability insurance), they should step down. And yet, no one likes to resign due to ignorance. Pride keeps them silent with heads nodding. It seems easier to trust the executives running the business. It seems easier to trust the accountants and lawyers—but in fact, one cannot conduct business without honest accountants and attorneys who respond to a free interplay of legitimate questions and answers.

Yet the elite team at Enron did not handle questions well, as shown by one of Skilling's infamous claims: "There are two kinds of people in the world—those who get it and those who don't."[3]

Note, too, that Ken Lay selected and molded Enron's board; the board did not handpick and scrutinize its chairman. Board members received way above average compensation and elaborate gifts from Lay, yet the chairman did not pay for any of the in-home entertainment or gifts he handed out; shareholders ponied up for all the luxurious perks that few of the directors would ever have lavished upon themselves.[4]

The Enron culture bred a sense of self-entitlement and fashionable opulence. The glory of this magnificent corporation apparently blinded the directors; they stood on the deck of the Titanic, believing it could never sink. T. S. Eliot, the Nobel Prize-winning twentieth-century poet, describes this state of mind: "Half of the harm that is done in this world is due to people who want to feel important. . . . They do not mean to do harm. . . . They are absorbed in the endless struggle to think well of themselves."[5]

Enron's directors surely did not want to see the signs of failure and doom just around the corner. They couldn't discern a problem even when asked to approve an exception to the corporate "Conflict of Interest Policy"—not the first time, nor even the second. Perhaps the second time felt easier because they had already given in once. In a theological sense, sin has a compounding effect; once compromises begin, it's difficult to get off the slippery slope and back on track.

In the end, the responsibility for Enron's demise lies with the members of the board, regardless of whether they purposely caused any of what happened.

What should a CEO expect from the board of directors? It's funny we should ask; Ken Lay penned a chapter with just that title in 1999. He said, "The responsibility of the board—a responsibility I expect them to fulfill—is to ensure legal and ethical conduct by the company and by everyone in the company." Lay wrote, "That requirement does not exist by happenstance. It is the most important thing we expect from board members."[6]

Mr. John Baugh, the highly respected Christian CEO who built Sysco Corporation, has said that his very first board of directors agreed that the "buck would stop at the board." As a result, every board member got a thorough education about Sysco to prevent the possibility of a director later squealing that he or she didn't understand what was going on. It is difficult, of course, to oversee a large corporation; but surely, someone on Enron's board could have stopped the train before it got too far off track.

FIGHTING A CONSTANT BATTLE

Must a full accounting be made of the Enron disaster? Surely. At the same time, however, these once highly esteemed directors, now in the autumn or winter of their lives, must find forgiveness for what happened during their watch. It behooves America, former Enroners, and shareholders to extend grace to those who allowed them to be harmed. Only in this way can we all begin a journey toward forgiveness and restoration.

How many of us, like former Enron employees, have a swagger in our walk? How many glow in the knowledge that others envy our status and position?

A dear friend and successful businessman described his own struggle with pride as "a constant battle. When I walk into a room, I am immediately sizing everyone up to see who is greater than or lesser than myself." Can you identify?

Pop psychology feeds our natural struggle with pride by focusing continually on our own problems and our journey toward self-actualization. Self-obsessed teens, who pander to their peers for attention and acceptance, commonly are thought to lack self-esteem (a synonym for self-love). In reality, they quite often struggle with pride and selfishness. If for only a few minutes they could get beyond themselves and reach out to another hurting human being, their own problems would fade into the background.

The business world is little different. Although few would ever admit it, many dominant CEOs often resemble timid schoolgirls; they seek acceptance and approval and live in constant fear of rejection. Even TV's top mob boss, Tony Soprano, worries incessantly that at some point his criminal and biological family will reject him. On the outside he seems like a formidable tough guy; on the inside he desperately longs for the approval of his mother and family.

Yet looking out for number one will always lead to the same place: isolation and loneliness. John, the apostle, said it this way: "Practically everything that goes on in the world—wanting your own way, wanting everything for yourself, wanting to appear important—has nothing to do with the Father. It just isolates you from him."[7] The great German reformer, Martin Luther, warns us in his *Larger Catechism,*

> Let them keep on boldly fleecing people as long as they can.
> God will not forget His commandment. He will pay them
> what they deserve. . . . Daily they leave the poor defrauded.
> New burdens and high prices are imposed. Everyone misuses
> the market in his own willful, conceited, arrogant way, as if it
> were his right and privilege to sell his goods as dearly as he
> pleased without a word of criticism. We shall stand by and
> let such persons fleece, grab, and hoard. But we shall trust
> God, who takes matters into his own hands. After they have
> scrimped and scraped for a long time, he will pronounce this
> kind of blessing over them: "Your grain will spoil in the gar-
> ner and your beer in the cellar. Your cattle will die in the
> stall. Yes, where you have cheated and defrauded anyone out
> of a gulden, your entire hoard will be consumed by rust so
> that you will never enjoy it."[8]

In his classic book *Mere Christianity,* C. S. Lewis cautions us to guard against pride and self-love: "According to Christian teachers, the essential vice, the utmost evil, is pride. Unchastity, anger, greed, drunkenness, and all that, are mere flea bites in comparison; it was through pride that the devil became the devil; pride leads to every other vice; it is the complete anti God state of mind."9

Pride is like a drug; it offers us an extreme high as we look down at the world. It comes easily with success and yet often shows up in failure. The Devil himself, as played by Al Pacino in *The Devil's Advocate*, says, "Pride — it's definitely my favorite sin!"

Practically speaking, pride prevents us from discovering and enjoying the very thing for which we were made: a buoyant relationship with God. Lewis writes,

> As long as you are proud you cannot know God. A proud
> man is always looking down on things and people: and, of
> course, as long as you are looking down, you cannot see
> something that is above you. That raises a terrible question.
> How is it that people who are quite obviously eaten up with
> pride can say they believe in God and appear to themselves
> very religious? I am afraid it means they are worshipping an
> imaginary God.10

So if pride causes such devastation, how can we ward it off? What's the antidote? Only one exists. Call it genuine humility.

A LIFE CENTERED IN THE CREATOR

Western culture, especially the culture of the U.S., does not associate the humble with the good. Even the best-selling *Book of Virtues* does not include humility as one of its ten vaunted character traits.

Humility flows from a life centered in our Creator; it cannot be found by seeking after itself. In fact, once we believe we have found humility, we have lost it. So what can we do to find it and embody it?

First, we must seek after spiritual truth and learn to be content in silence. Richard Foster, in his classic *Celebration of Discipline*, writes, "Humility, as we all know, is one of those virtues that is never gained by seeking it. The more we pursue it the more distant it becomes. To think we have it is sure evidence that we don't. Therefore, most of us assume there is nothing we can do to obtain this prized Christian virtue so we do nothing."[11]

Unlike so many who know what to preach against but offer little hope for change, Foster suggests a course of action for those who desire the virtue of humility. As a caution, Foster points out that "arrogance and a teachable spirit are mutually exclusive."[12] He then says, "Isn't it sad for society that often times the very intelligent people, the ones who could contribute the most to the world, are the ones least teachable? Since they consider themselves better than others, from whom would they learn?" Foster continues,

> We do not need to go through life faintly hoping that some-day humility may fall upon our heads. Of all the classical Spiritual Disciplines, service is the most conducive to the growth of humility. When we set out on a consciously chosen course of action that accents the good of others and is, for the most part, a hidden work, a deep change occurs in our spirits.[13]

That "deep change in our spirits" enables us to reject pride and all the deadly baggage that travels with it. At the same time it permits us to enjoy the satisfaction and fulfillment that we all desire as we humbly act for the benefit of others. Such a life leads to celebration and avoids crippling remorse.

Like he so often does, Jesus sums it up best. "If you puff yourself up," said the Son of Man, "you'll get the wind knocked out of you. But if you're content to simply be yourself, your life will count for plenty."[14]

CHAPTER 7

Rebecca Mark: Rise to the Top

In America's highly aggressive, chauvinist business culture, Rebecca Mark seemed an unlikely candidate for CEO and president of Azurix, the water utility subsidiary of the company leading the way in the "New Economy." Even she commented, "Quite a journey for a simple farm girl, hey?"[1]

And she's right about at least one thing: She did begin as a simple farm girl before becoming one of the most respected—and feared—women in corporate America.

NO EARLY SIGNS

Rebecca Mark grew up on her family's farm in Kirksville, Missouri, just as her ancestors before her. The second of two children in a strict Baptist family, she felt drawn to books and languages. No one seems to have noticed early signs of her future as "Mark the Shark," the bane of the boardroom.

Joellen Hayes, the librarian at Kirksville High School, remembers Rebecca as "not terribly outgoing—more quiet and reserved."[2] Mark's choice of college also didn't suggest the rule breaker and deal maker she was to become. She majored in psychology at Baylor University in Waco, Texas, partially out of consideration for her parents, who, Rebecca admits, "thought I'd be much safer in a conservative town."[3]

Mark began to change into "the shark" in 1978 when she entered a training program at a large bank in Houston that serviced loans to several energy companies—her first step in becoming the forceful queen of an energy empire. In 1982, Mark joined the treasury department at Continental Resources, a natural gas pipeline company eventually acquired by Houston Natural Gas (the precursor to Enron) in 1985. At that time she was married to Thomas Mark, with whom she had a set of twins. In 1988 their marriage ended in divorce and Rebecca gained custody of their sons. After the divorce, she reduced her work at Enron to part-time while she pursued a master's degree in international management at Harvard Business School, adroitly juggling motherhood, school, and career.

Soon after Mark completed her degree at Harvard and returned full-time to Enron, she convinced company chairman and CEO Ken Lay of the vast possibilities for growth and expansion to be found in international arenas. So in 1991, Enron created Enron Development Corporation to seek out global opportunities. Mark became CEO of the newborn corporation. She quickly became a celebrity and earned for herself the title "Mark the Shark" as an aggressive negotiator and ruthless businesswoman who could sell ice to Eskimos.

In his book *Pipe Dreams: Greed, Ego, and the Death of Enron*, Robert Bryce describes Rebecca as "a size-six bottle blonde with high cheekbones, extra-straight, extra-big, extra-white teeth, enormous brown eyes and always perfect makeup." Unlike other businesswomen who tend to adhere to the corporate dress code of a conservative suit, she always dressed to the nines in a look Bryce calls, "very upscale yet slightly trampy," with outfits from Armani and Escada, "usually including miniskirts and a pair of comehither stiletto heels."[4]

Another commentator adds that Mark, "was aware and confident of her good looks. Nor did she make any apologies about using her femininity as a professional asset. Then and now, she dresses to kill, having given up long ago the formal female corporate attire."[5] Mark, labeled "one of the most authoritative and strikingly successful businesswomen in the United States," ambled through the world of business, drawing attention for her good looks and her ambition.[6]

HEADING TOWARD THE TOP

Mark soon conquered Enron, coming very close to the golden ring of CEO-ship. Judged purely on her compensation, it seemed clear that she was going someplace—and that place looked like the very top.

According to Robert Bryce,

> Company proxies show that between 1996 and 1998, her total compensation was $25.7 million—that's more than any other Enron employee during that time, including Ken Lay ($16.7 million) and Jeff Skilling ($25.4 million). By 1998, she was named vice chairman of the Enron board and held voting power on more stock than anyone else on the board except for Robert Belfer—a director who lost 1 billion dollars—Lay and Skilling. Despite her wealth of assets, Enron began treating Mark like a favored third-world country. In 1998, Enron's compensation committee forgave all of the principal and interest on a $955,343 loan the company had granted her in 1997. In early 1999, Enron did even

more, pardoning an additional $700,000 loan the company made to her in 1998.[7]

For good reason people called her "Hell in High Heels." As Brian Cruver, an Enron insider, put it, "With jet-powered high heels and her blond hair blowing in the wind, she developed international power projects from Bombay to the Philippines."[8]

Rebecca made her mark in the business world with the Dabhol power project in India, a venture set up and managed under Enron International, which the company began in 1993 with her at the helm. She pulled Dabhol from the ashes in 1996 and earned major worldwide recognition, including a place on the cover of *Fortune* magazine.

Mark proposed the construction of a 2,015-megawatt power plant that would cost about $2.9 billion, a deal with countless financial and political obstacles. But after years of development and negotiating, Mark pulled it off, "shepherding the project through a turbulent political and bureaucratic maze" and winning more acclaim from her business peers, as well as global esteem as a woman of achievement.[9]

Still, Dabhol eventually turned into a disaster. Enron had to shut down the plant in May 2001 for lack of funds; the Indian people could not afford the electricity Dabhol generated and so the company could not sustain itself.

Next, Mark turned toward developing another market within which Enron could lead the way: acquiring and distributing water. In 1998, Enron began Azurix, the company's first and only water utility company, with Mark serving as chairman of the board and chief executive officer. In her first move as CEO of Azurix, Mark negotiated the purchase of Britain's Wessex Water, a deal worth over $2.5 billion. Enron went public with Azurix in 1999, but under Mark's leadership, "the would-be global water company quickly over-extended itself with capital-intensive and trouble-plagued acquisitions."[10]

Again, Enron and Mark's ideas and investments proved insufficient to the challenge. Azurix could not support itself and finally drowned Mark's reputation. Feeling the pressure of expensive and highly visible failures—and the ongoing enmity of Jeff Skilling, her rival for future power at Enron—in August 2000, Rebecca Mark resigned as CEO of Azurix and as a board member of Enron.

In some ways, Mark got pushed out of the tower because of her adherence to the old market idea that assets still counted for something. In the culture of now-not-later that became Enron, forward-looking deals and present-time losses became unacceptable.

NO VERDICT YET

The jury is still out on Rebecca Mark. While many criticized her personal style and her business acumen—some business analysts suggest that her considerable skill as CEO came in conception and presentation, rather than in operation—she also risked her position by daring to declare unpopular ideas.

Even after John Wing, one of Mark's key allies, left the firm, Mark had the guts to confront her old friend Ken Lay in a meeting where she informed him, "You are being snookered. . . . These are profits from the sale of assets. These are not trading profits."[11] Too late: Skilling was piloting the ship, and by that time Lay reportedly looked at Mark with condescension.

Despite her short skirts and high heels, Rebecca Mark had become a dinosaur. "Her assets, at best, could return 14 percent, but she was planning for the long run with equity investments, a strategy designed to hold an investment for decades," Marie Brenner notes, "and the company had veered inexorably toward the culture of traders, where profits now soared to close to 30 percent every year."[12]

What did it matter that those profits were hardly more real than Monopoly money? You could still seize it and spend it. And spend it they did . . . until it had all vanished.

LESSONS FROM A RISE AND FALL

We can learn some obvious lessons from Ms. Mark's rise and fall.

First, I think of the old proverb about using a long spoon if you're going to sup with the Devil. Given Mark's background and history, I prefer another, more modern aphorism: If you're going to swim with the sharks, don't be surprised when you get bit.

Second, if you make rising to the top your primary goal, understand that your rivals will make your sinking *their* top priority.

Third, while it's possible to make excessive amounts of money even through failed business ventures, it's not possible to do so without swimming in some pretty foul waters—and the vile exercise always leaves behind an overpowering stench that refuses to go away.

Rebecca Mark had the good fortune to get pushed out of Enron before the Death Star exploded, so in some ways she enjoyed a cushioned descent. But still, for the former farm girl turned corporate storm trooper, the fall had to sting.

CHAPTER 8

A Lust for Power

If human beings covet anything more than wealth, it is power.

Why else would someone like Ross Perot spend millions of dollars in a long-shot attempt to land himself in the most powerful office in the world? Why else would famous Hollywood stars give up thriving cinematic careers to seek public office? And why else would Enron executives risk everything, except in a bid for unrestrained, unfettered power?

MASTERS OF THE UNIVERSE

The men and women at Enron were supposed to be the best and brightest; they considered themselves the masters of the universe. They had graduated from the best schools, studied the latest theories, and spearheaded corporate innovation. Their leader, Kenneth Lay, held a Ph.D. in economics. They thought their knowledge put them above regulation and ethics. They even thought themselves above other geniuses.

When Jeff Skilling brought Andrew Fastow's plan for counting hundreds of millions of dollars of profit — from an Enron investment in an Internet start-up called Rhythms NetConnections — to Enron financial analyst Vince Kaminski, Kaminski could hardly believe what he saw. And when Kaminski took the Skilling/Fastow idea (another of those ubiquitous partnership arrangements) back to his team, "world-class mathematicians who used arcane statistical models to analyze risk—the room exploded in laughter." It was an idea so stupid, Kaminski thought, that only Andrew Fastow could have come up with it.[1]

Nonetheless, Enron ran with the idea, Fastow personally made millions of dollars from managing the partnership, and with a few breaks here and there, Fastow and Skilling's rule-bending genius might even have let them dodge disaster.

At Enron, as in much of corporate America, what was deemed important was one's rise to the top—not *how* one got there. So an "important former executive at Enron" could say admiringly of Rebecca Mark, "She's as good with her sexuality around men as anyone I've ever seen. She knows how to flaunt it. She just knew how to use her intelligence and sexuality to her advantage."[2]

But this lust for power didn't stop with wobbly business deals. Not when larger avenues of influence lay open in the august halls of Congress.

THE MAGICAL POWER OF WEALTH

Wealth doesn't merely create personal convenience and lavish lifestyles; it also grants the bearer almost magical powers to buy influence.

Many consider the greatest flaw of American democracy to be the ability of wealthy individuals and powerful corporations to wield awesome influence over the laws that govern our society (as well as over the leaders themselves). Despite recent passage of legislation reforming campaign finance, wealth still grants the givers incredible privilege and access to lawmakers and executives.

I can't afford to give $100,000 to the Republican Party, so I count my chances of ever having a heart to heart with George W. Bush as slim to none. But if somehow I had the money to make such a sizeable contribution, I might very well get invited to sit with him at a breakfast, or spend time with him and other prominent politicians at a private retreat, or even help to write legislation governing my business.

So is this strictly a Republican thing? Hardly. Things worked no differently under the Democrats. Remember Bill Clinton "selling" nights in the White House's Lincoln Bedroom to big contributors?

The point is both simple and bipartisan: Big money has access to power that can change the rules for those with big money—and Enron, of course, remains a prime example.

The sight of investigators, our attorney general, and various members of Congress recusing themselves from hearings on Enron—or admitting to receiving large contributions from Enron—sobered us all. Then-Governor George W. Bush counted Kenneth Lay as one of his most enthusiastic supporters; Lay hopped on the Bush-for-President bandwagon before it had wheels. And Lay and Enron have remained Bush's largest single donor to this point in his political career.

Nevertheless, that financial support didn't ultimately save Enron—the Bush administration rightly ignored Lay's calls for a last minute bailout—but it did buy the company incredible access and policy influence. At the time of this writing, investigators are still seeking Vice President Cheney's records of meetings with energy moguls where the Bush energy policy (heavy on deregulation and fossil fuels, light on conservation and alternative energy) got hammered out.

What kind of nation do we live in, I wonder, when industry lobbyists and tycoons can actively shape the writing of legislation that will govern their industries? To what have we descended when Wendy

Gramm, wife of powerful Senator Phil Gramm (R, Texas), can serve on the board of Enron while the company makes huge contributions to her husband—a man who will then vote on legislation concerning the company? What has happened when President Bush's chief advisor, Karl Rove, can hold Enron stock while deliberating the energy policy Enron helped write?

Isn't it clear to us yet that such power is wrong, that it subverts democracy, that it leads to government by the wealthy for the wealthy? Jack Beatty concluded his discussion of politicians and other figures who may have been influenced by Enron's cash in this way:

> Did Enroning secure the silence of the Administration
> officials — the Treasury Secretary, the Commerce Secretary,
> the President's Chief Economic Advisor, and the President's
> Chief of Staff—who knew Enron was on the ropes last fall
> [2001] but said nothing to the Securities and Exchange
> Commission or the public? They said nothing while state
> pension funds were losing $2.9 billion on a company legiti-
> mated by an Enroned board, blessed by Enroned lawyers,
> pronounced robust by Enroned accountants, and hailed as a
> "strong buy" right up until the eve of its bankruptcy by
> Enroned investment bankers.[3]

Is there substance to Beatty's questions? The court proceedings that must inevitably follow may give us some answers. But even before then, we know one thing for sure: When big money buys big influence, power begins to flow along greenback-lined channels—and lots of people get hurt.

ON WHOSE SIDE IS GOD?

At Enron, money talked. We've witnessed how the big producers got what they wanted and how a significant percentage of Enron employees got reassigned or fired based on arbitrary ratings.

In fact, the Performance Review Committees at Enron demonstrate one of the most brutish exercises of power. Robert Bryce wrote that the PRCs "allowed people with power to punish or threaten their enemies, and it created enormous incentives to push through deals that were bad for the company but very good for the individuals." All this power lay in the hands of the dealmakers; Bryce said that the people who actually performed the work of Enron "got crushed by this rolling egomaniac culture. But if you were a 'revenue generator,' you were God."[4]

Well, not any god who I ever knew. Archbishop Desmond Tutu has argued throughout his courageous career that God doesn't take the side of the rich and powerful. From the Hebrew Bible's emphasis on justice and mercy to Christ's calls for generosity and his message to the rich young ruler to renounce his wealth if he meant to follow Jesus, the Bible is clear: "God can't help it. He always takes sides. He is no neutral God. He takes the side of the weak and the oppressed. . . . Where there is injustice, exploitation and oppression, then, the Bible and the God of the Bible are subversive of such a situation. . . . He is a God of surprises, uprooting the powerful and unjust to establish his Kingdom."[5]

Does this mean that God condemns power? That power is necessarily evil? We must reject any such conclusion. The story of Joseph in the book of Genesis provides one example (among many) of how to use power with wisdom and love to achieve an ultimate good.[6]

But the Bible also contains dozens of examples of power gone wrong, examples that show us how the love of power will begin a never-ending cycle that leads a soul to loneliness and desperation.[7]

Although we are creations of God, we continually strive to *be* God and to gain ultimate power. The lust for power is not peculiar to corporate America; it's a distinctively human failing.

The assistant manager at Baskin Robbins is as likely to deceive and scheme to obtain the coveted office of manager as any corporate scoundrel behind a multibillion-dollar business takeover. And if thwarted in that scheme, Mr. Baskin Robbins will still come home and lord it over his wife and kids. And the youngest and most powerless of those kids will order the dog to go sit in the corner or arrange her dolls in a row and command them to do her bidding.

THE ULTIMATE APHRODISIAC

Power has been described as the ultimate aphrodisiac. Most of us feel irresistibly drawn to dominant personalities and influential decision makers. Many paths lead to power, including knowledge, great wealth, and brute strength, and it's important for us to know about all of them—and to be wary of falling under their spell.

Sin was birthed in this universe through a desire for knowledge that would make us like God[8]—and the path of modern society has brought this evil desire to its ultimate conclusion. The arrival of modernity spawned many opportunities to explain and master the universe. The scientific theory promised unadulterated truth in the natural sciences, mathematics, the study of man, and theology. As one of the proverbs goes, "God delights in concealing things; scientists delight in discovering things."[9]

Throughout history, governments and individuals have ravaged their neighbors by means of brute strength. Intelligence, money, and power can run roughshod over most things in their way. Nations seek to oppress weaker nations; slavery gets justified, even by people of faith; governments stockpile enough weapons to destroy the entire planet several times over; and educated businesspeople abandon their moral compasses at the mere scent of a lucrative promotion.

Still, as we've said, power is not evil by nature. In fact, the Bible instructs us to obey those in authority. The problem with power comes when we seek it as a means to feed our own egos and go after our own desires.

Is that your motivation, to seek positions of power and influence? Just what are you willing to do in order to gain authority and influence? Are you willing to degrade other employees whom you consider a threat to your advancement; take credit for work that is not your own; or buy, barter, or sleep your way to the top? Many executives have destroyed their credibility and capacity to lead because of the way they achieved their positions. Honor cannot easily be restored; reputations that take decades to build can go up in smoke over a period of days, if not hours.

Jesus warned us, "You've observed how godless rulers throw their weight around . . . and when people get a little power how quickly it goes to their heads."[10] If Enron has taught us nothing else, it certainly has taught us *that*.

IT COMES DOWN TO THIS

We Americans have greatly distorted views of power, authority, and control. We think it a noble (if novel) thought when the movie and comic book hero Spiderman learns that, "With great power comes great responsibility."

It may seem a daunting task to oversee others who trust your leadership and integrity. But it comes down to this: Great leaders care for people and make their lives easier while poor leaders bring devastation to all who follow them. If you can't stand the heat — if you can't lead with wisdom and justice and integrity — then get out of the leadership kitchen.

The Hebrew Scriptures insist on the great responsibility of the king and instruct him that "Leaders can't afford to make fools of themselves, gulping wine and swilling beer, lest, hung over, they don't know right from wrong, and the people who depend on them are hurt."[11] They also remind us that the Bible "is to remain at his side at all times; he is to study it every day so that he may learn what it means to fear his GOD, living in reverent obedience before these rules and regulations by following them."[12]

More important than studying the will and Word of God, however, is to practice it. And if the leaders of Enron — even those who call themselves people of faith — had done this, then their power could have created good in the world instead of the moral black hole that doomed their company, rocked the economy, and hurt investors around the globe.

We must remember this: Only the creator of heaven and earth holds ultimate power. He blesses those who lead as servants, giving freely of what they have. In the words of a great leader and apostle, "In everything I've done, I have demonstrated to you how necessary it is to work on behalf of the weak and not exploit them. You'll not likely go wrong here if you keep remembering that our Master said, 'You're far happier giving than getting.'"[13]

And even better yet, your happiness will spill over into the lives of those you lead.

CHAPTER 9

Andrew Fastow: A Portrait of Impatience

CFO magazine selected Andrew Fastow as a 1999 Excellence Award Winner for Capital Structure Management, honoring him as one of the "Finest in Finance."[1] Only three years later, times had changed. Another *CFO* article on Fastow grimly read, "Former Enron CFO Fastow surrenders to FBI, dons a new pair of cuffs."[2]

Like Jeffrey Skilling, his mentor, Fastow soared to the top of the corporate world, then plunged to the depths of disgrace. Fastow was the "boy genius" behind Enron's many and complex financial deals, lauded as one who helped transform Enron from "an old gas-pipeline culture into a swaggering, rule-breaking, deal-making cult."[3] Ultimately, he served as the greatest emblem of the corporation's willingness to bend the rules and mortgage the future to achieve instant gratification.

RISING WITH HIS BOSS

Andrew Fastow grew up in New Jersey, graduated from Tufts University in 1983 with a BA in Chinese and economics, and went on to Northwestern University, where in 1986 he earned his MBA. He met his wife, Lea Weingarten, at Tufts and married into considerable wealth: the Weingartens owned upward of eighty grocery stores and held an honored place as one of Houston's best-known Jewish families.

After graduation, Fastow worked at Continental Illinois Bank from 1984 to 1990, where he mastered the art of increasingly convoluted accounting deals. Then in 1990, he joined Enron Corp. as a managing director with Enron Capital Trade Resources. There he developed a close working relationship with executive Jeffrey Skilling, rising in the company as his boss rose. In 1996, Fastow—still only in his mid-thirties—took over Enron's retail energy business. With Skilling's backing, he became CFO of Enron in 1998. A year later, he became executive vice president.

During his early years with Skilling, Fastow is alleged to have designed the limited partnerships that Enron employed to maximize its profits and camouflage its debts from creditors and shareholders. As his skill grew at constructing these complicated arrangements, so did his fame. "Fastow quickly earned a reputation as a money wizard who constructed the complex financial vehicles that Enron drove on the road to explosive growth."[4]

Jan Avery, who worked in accounting at Enron, recalls a conference in 1995 where Fastow stood in front of a white board dotted with circles representing partnerships (three hundred or so already existed), brainstorming with those in attendance about ways to shuffle debts around and "maintain the value"—Enron accounting lingo for "hiding a loss." In and of itself, the procedure was not illegal. "It was still within the realm of accounting rules," Avery said. Nevertheless, it was clearly wrong and it "became criminal when they continued it to such a degree that it put all the shareholders at risk."[5]

As Enron moved from an asset-model, old-economy business to a trading-model, new-economy business, its major executives became more and more shortsighted. They wanted money—in fact, had to have loads of it—and they wanted it *now*. Andrew Fastow was the man they had hired to make that happen. The court is investigating Fastow's alleged use of off-balance accounting, deceit, and innumerable allegedly crooked deals, which helped create the mechanisms Enron needed to find instant satisfaction.[6]

In its final years, Enron bloated its ledger (and fooled those wanting an accurate value of the company) primarily through the adoption of "mark to marketing" accounting. Under this nontraditional accounting model—again, not technically illegal, although it now seems clear that the company abused this accounting gray area to the extent of illegality—Enron booked as initial-year profit *any* profit it expected to realize from multiyear deals. It even set the level of profit it expected to make, wildly inflating its estimates.

Of course, as Enron continued to conceal its losses and seize long-term profits to pay its then-current bills, it ceased to be a viable company. It ate up all its cash reserves and relied on bigger and bigger deals to increase its profit statements and keep its stock value high.

Ultimately, we may discover that Enron had neither the ability nor the intention of providing what it had promised to its customers. Even when customers backed out of deals with the explanation that they no longer seemed profitable enough at least Enron gained some money in hand. The deal had been done. Mission complete.

And as CFO, Fastow played a central role in Enron's grab for cash.

Fastow served as the company's chief financial officer—at least in name—from May 1998 until his termination in October 2001 by the company's board of directors. During the last years of the corporation, Enron's top tax attorney, Robert J. Hermann, watched the gap between the profit demands of upper management and the sums division managers believed they could generate grow further and further apart. It became apparent to him that Fastow was not a "real CFO." Fastow and his partners seemed interested only in what they could grab at the moment.

Here's how Hermann summed up the Enron fiasco: "I realized that there was nobody doing any planning in that company. . . . They were just managing it day to day and trying to get earnings for the quarter."[7]

Live for today. Who cares about tomorrow? I want it. *Now.*

To this the Psalms prophetically declare, "Their greed knew no bounds; they stuffed their mouths with more and more."[8] And Jesus concludes, "If you live squinty-eyed in greed and distrust, your body is a dank cellar. If you pull the blinds on your windows, what a dark life you will have!"[9]

TREMENDOUS PERSONAL COST

Who could blame young Andrew for believing that all good things in life should be handed to him on a silver platter? It seemed to be working.

He had risen to a level of untold corporate success and riches before his fortieth birthday. He served as the chief financial officer for a company that his friend, Jeffrey Skilling, liked to describe as the hottest, smartest, sexiest, most dynamic corporation in the world.

But even this instant gratification came at a tremendous cost—and not just to the shareholders, debtors, and others who would face financial ruin through Fastow's decisions. It also came at a tremendous spiritual cost to *him.* Jack Beatty, writing in the on-line version of *The Atlantic*, made the moral dimension clear:

You are Andrew Fastow, Enron's CFO, and you have this problem. You have set up more than 3,000 partnerships to hide Enron's losses of more than $500,000,000. An Enron controller is pressing you on the unsavory details of your scheme. You get him transferred. His replacement you cut in on the deal. He gives you $5,000 to invest in one of the partnerships and two months later gets a $1,000,000 return. Your problem has disappeared. You have snared him in what we might call an Enron. You yourself are mega-Enroned, as overseer and beneficiary of partnerships from which you have gained 30 million dollars.[10]

Magnify this event by every problem, every lie, every manipulation, and you can see the staggering soul cost of instant gratification.

"Practically everything that goes on in the world—wanting your own way, wanting everything for yourself, wanting to appear important—has nothing to do with the Father," warns the apostle John. "It just isolates you from him."[11]

GAIN THE WORLD, LOSE YOUR SOUL

What does it profit a man, Jesus asked, to gain the whole world, and lose his soul?[12] It is a question that could be asked of many of Enron's top executives.

For Fastow, who is facing charges that if convicted require a century and a half in jail, the fall has been long and fast; but whether it has served to awaken in him a moral sensibility remains to be seen. His refusals to cooperate with the Securities and Exchange Commission, with the congressional committees investigating

Enron's collapse, and with the Justice Department do not bode well for an acceptance of responsibility.

One fired Enron employee described a post-meltdown encounter with Fastow in a Houston sushi restaurant: "Fastow looked relaxed and happy. It even seemed like he enjoyed the fact that everyone in the restaurant was staring at him."[13]

Andrew Fastow's rabbi once said of him, "You'd never even know what he did for a living."[14]

At least, not until his day in court.

CHAPTER 10

I Want It Now

Why is it that nearly all of our popular maxims about wealth seem to speak of urgency and impatience?

- "Get rich quick."
- "Win the lotto."
- "Grab for the gusto."
- "Use it or lose it."
- "Get it before it's gone."

When did you ever hear someone say he was trying to "get rich slow"?

Great wealth seduces. It calls out to all of us, promising a life filled with pleasures of every kind, the praise of man, knowledge that will open every door, and a remedy for loneliness and isolation. And it declares urgently, "Take it now or lose it forever."

Many of the top managers at Enron serve as poster children for impatience—and not only because they heard the siren call of big money. With Enron's live-for-today accounting, they really felt as though if they didn't cash in right away, it would be too late.

THE LINK BETWEEN IMPATIENCE AND GREED

Enron built its whole business strategy on leveraging assets to create profits. *Now.*

The company regularly illustrated the poisonous link between impatience and greed. At least one member of its human resources department, for example, had to become proficient in dealing with "compensation emergencies."

Businesspeople don't normally think of an employee's salary and incentives as items to be handled on the same afternoon that an executive discovers a need for "emergency treatment." But at Enron, human resources personnel commonly dropped everything in order to revise a prized employee's contract terms before that employee left for home that night. Like the huge cash advances and corporate loans to Enron executives (who already had been richly compensated), the frequent "compensation emergencies" reflected an astonishing corporate impatience.

What would happen, do you think, if you went to your employer (or shareholders) to demand a change in your compensation package, an alteration that you insisted couldn't wait overnight? I'd be willing to bet that however well regarded you might be, you'd find that your demands would have to wait until at least the next day.

At Enron, however, the terms of previous employment agreements—no matter how recently hammered out—gave license to leverage better deals through "emergency contracts." These deals had to be completed immediately, executives thought, or the prized employee might accept an offer from a competitor. And so impatience led to bad behavior on both the personal and company levels.

WHEN LOANS EXCEED INCOME

In the simplest of terms, Enron collapsed because it borrowed more money than it could pay back. As money walked in the front door, it walked out the back door—or more likely, sped out of the parking garage in an executive's sleek new Porsche or Mercedes.

As long as Enron's stock remained above twenty dollars a share, investors eagerly placed their faith in the company's creditworthiness. Meanwhile, corporate executives labored to forge a network of shady deals, faulty accounting, and slick salesmanship to keep the company afloat for another quarter.

But of course, the whole sham collapsed in the end. The energy market, the high-tech bust, and whispers about Andrew Fastow's huge profits from his off-balance-sheet partnerships started the crash. Eventually, Enron's bubble had to burst.

To mix metaphors, you can't keep a ship afloat when more water pours in than the pumps can bail out. The situation at Enron might still have been saved, Robert Bryce suggests, if Ken Lay had opened the doors to the SEC, halted trading of company stocks, and dealt honestly with the problem. He didn't.

And great was the company's fall.

DISHONESTY OR INCOMPETENCE?

So who was most at fault? No one yet has stepped forward to accept blame.

To this day, senior Enron attorneys, senior tax officers, senior accounting officers, independent outside auditors, members of the board of directors, members of Wall Street, and even the chairman of the board and short-term chief executive officer all claim they acted honestly. According to Enron's corporate tax lawyer, Robert J. Hermann, Lay told Enron's top management on October 22, 2001, "Well, we don't think we did anything wrong, but knowing what we do now, we would never do it again."[1]

Jeff Skilling testified before Congress that he, like Ken Lay, knew of no "financing arrangements designed to conceal liabilities or inflate profitability." He claimed that until informed otherwise, he believed Enron was "in strong financial shape."[2]

At the time of this writing all these individuals still proclaimed their innocence, and until and unless their claims get disproved in court, they are entitled to such a consideration.[3] Still, we cannot neglect to consider other alternatives.

Was the collapse of Enron primarily an issue of incompetency? Is it possible that the Enron strategy, developed by some of the top business and accounting minds in America, suffered from cataclysmic and irredeemable flaws? That certainly seems to be at least partly the case.

Enron executed a financial strategy based on leveraging all its assets to maximize profit—and it's not alone. Many individuals and corporations take a similar risk. Investors buy stock on margin while entrepreneurs start businesses with high-risk credit card debt.

The question regarding Enron is this: Would an honest *and* competent group take the kind of risks that might well lead a corporation into sudden and complete collapse? Would not honest *and* competent executives and board members insist on holding on to something of solid value, a hard asset that, working with our nation's generous bankruptcy laws, might allow the incubation of some sort of phoenix? Did Enron have such confidence in its "coolness" that it consciously adopted a "live-outside-the-envelope, do-or-die" philosophy?

Because business often requires taking extreme risk (to a greater or lesser degree), it may be time to redefine the nature of competency in corporate boardrooms. Something must be done to prevent managers from looting the corporations under their watch. Perhaps reform needs to begin with the board of directors.

But back to Enron. In the case of its board, only a few options present themselves:

- The board maximized risk for the sake of profits.
- The board was completely duped.
- The board offered a textbook example of incompetence.

To claim ignorance, as board members universally have done, is simply unconscionable. The investing public has a far better claim for being misled than the board. The board's own audit committee expressed its satisfaction that management had done everything necessary to properly manage Enron's devastating debt.

Why didn't a single member of the board take issue with the amount of debt and the way it was being disclosed in the fine print? Couldn't even one director see the iceberg looming ahead?

Just as the government requires drug manufacturers to publicize possible side effects of their products, corporations should be required to fully disclose their total debt—and in LARGE PRINT. If legislators find it impossible to change current accounting standards, then perhaps individual board members should begin to demand that they receive monthly updates on total debt, regardless of which balance sheet, partnership, or foreign subsidiary is involved.

Unfortunately, honesty and integrity cannot be legislated—and in the wake of Enron and similar scandals, those qualities in the corporate world seem increasingly scarce.

A WORKING DEFINITION

Because a "minister of the gospel" should never say that someone lacks integrity without first defining the term, let me try out a working definition. "Integrity" does not imply perfection, because no person goes through this life blameless. People of integrity, however, do make their best efforts to communicate the truth. People of integrity live in a way consistent with their words (whether or not they speak under oath). They do not put a spin on their statements, nor do they take pains to create loopholes through which they may slither. Their yes means yes, and their no, no. And when they do not know, they say that, as well.

We might imagine that some folks at Enron had about as much to do with this kind of integrity as Bing Crosby did with gangsta rap. But did you know that Enron publicly listed "integrity" as one of its four core values (along with respect, communication, and excellence)? Listen to the official rhetoric:

> *Integrity.* We work with customers and prospects openly, honestly, and sincerely. When we say we will do something, we will do it; when we say we cannot or will not do something, then we won't do it.[4]

It sounds great, doesn't it? Who wouldn't want to work with a group that champions open, honest, and sincere business practices? Who wouldn't trust a company that does what it says it will do and refuses to do what it says it won't do? Who, indeed? Integrity is a fabulous thing.

That is, so long as it truly exists—and there's the rub.

IMPATIENCE LEADS TO LOSS OF INTEGRITY

When impatience ascends the throne, integrity goes into exile. The two cannot coexist.

Despite the many honest executives, workers, and board members who populate today's business world, too many college students join companies and a system that lack even a vestige of integrity. How can integrity be restored to business? How can a lack of honesty be recognized and avoided?

Fortunately, there are clues.

For example, anyone who misrepresents herself or himself on a résumé or employment application lacks integrity. Such employees should be dumped before they can reach a position in which they can do real damage.

A retired CEO who built a still-thriving company once said he always felt wary of men who divorced their wives. Rightly or not, he believed that a man who would double-cross his own children couldn't be trusted with shareholder assets. His single guideline, if applied at Enron, would have eliminated more than a few executives—and potentially saved thousands of investors billions of dollars.

Don't get me wrong. I don't want to leap to some kind of self-righteous, moralistic judgment here. But we would all do well to remember Jesus' statement that, "by their fruit you will recognize them."[5]

And all of us have some fruit that should have landed in the compost heap years ago.

It's oh so easy to blame others. Often, we too are guilty of (as the Anglican Prayer Book puts it) sins of omission as well as sins of commission. When Dr. Martin Luther King Jr. considered the South in the 1950s, for example, he directed his harshest words not to the bigots, to the Klan members, or to the political opponents of the Civil Rights movement, but to the church. His heart breaking, he told white clergy in his famous *Letter from a Birmingham Jail* that "we will have to repent in this generation not merely for the vitriolic words and actions of the bad people, but for the appalling silence of the good people."[6]

In a new book awaiting publication, Dr. John Neesley echoes King with an important question for those concerned over ethics in the workplace: "Are you covering up ethical violations of others?" And he offers one suggestion for reflection: "Silence may be golden, or it may be just plain yellow. We may be too frightened to confront someone with truth."

If Dr. Neesley's comment rings true with us, it sounds doubly true for an unstable house of cards like Enron.

WHERE WERE THE WHISTLES?

From Enron's highest levels on down, those in positions of responsibility frowned on questions about debt structuring, challenges, and even the specter of loss. Many of those in power had nasty tempers and low flash points.

Some kept silent for fear of losing their jobs. The top spots at Enron featured compensation packages that made walking away difficult. Even the multitude of bright young MBAs knew their Enron paychecks far outstripped anything they might receive at a competing company.

At some point, compensation can cross the line from payment for work and reward for exceptional performance to a form of bribery. In an environment where facts bring little appreciation and truth can have a devastating impact on the price of company stock, outrageous compensation begins to distort personal values.

Other factors besides the substantial pay prompted some at the top to stay on and stay silent. Simply put, they loved the freedom. They operated with great liberty to do whatever they wanted. Whenever a "bureaucrat" questioned a decision by one of the Enron elite, he or she invariably got slapped down for not appreciating the freedom required to move outside the envelope.

Former employees give many reasons for not stepping forward. Consider just a few:

• Concern for job security
• Fear over loss of lifestyle
• Possible complicity in questionable activities
• The rationalization that "Everybody does it"

Whatever the reasons, many employees realized that to make it at Enron, they had to sell at least a bit of their souls. "We've all got to drink the Kool-Aid," a high-ranking Enron exec said after the big bosses told him to "do a bogus deal."[7] So they drank heartily.

To cover their tracks, they began to spin negative information, put crucial details in fine print, or suppress unfortunate facts altogether. "Investor relations personnel" were hired to promote good news so tenaciously that Wall Street analysts could be persuaded that any rotting parts of the corporation could easily be forgotten in view of the company's pulsating muscle. Enron appears to have effectively pressured at least one brave analyst out of his job when he could not bring himself to see the quality shining through the putrefying corpse before him.[8]

It should be noted, too, that some employees failed to blow their whistles because much of what took place at Enron could actually be construed as legal. "Aggressive" and "out there" accounting? Certainly. But somehow it remained possible for the Arthur Andersen accounting firm and Enron's expert lawyers to contend that the company's wizards of the books had not violated the law.

These outrageous practices permitted Enron to operate what some analysts have called a giant Ponzi scheme. Those who impatiently got in and out early made (or took) the money; millions more found their pockets turned out.

How can our system allow a few investors to walk away with tens of millions of dollars while the vast majority of others lose their retirement incomes and life savings? Ken, Jeff, Rebecca, and many other top executives are now millionaires many times over, while shareholders—the legal owners of the company—own worthless stock certificates good only for show-and-tell. To worsen the pain and insult, bankruptcy lawyers rake in millions each month while newly penniless retirees wonder what they will do without the nest eggs Enron promised them.

When the wife of Ken Lay—a man so trusted by many investors that they held on to their stocks even after Skilling departed—goes on national television to describe their loss, frustration, and fears of losing their seventeen-thousand-square-foot home, it is hard for the public to empathize. It is even harder for them to empathize when they read in *Mother Jones* magazine that, starting in 2007, the Lays will receive a guaranteed annual income of about $900,000, made possible through a variable annuity they purchased in February 2000—an investment "virtually impervious to attack by creditors."[9]

The frustration that many feel today prompts questions a good deal like those expressed by the lamenting prophet Jeremiah, who questioned God over the outrages of his own generation:

You are always righteous O LORD,

    when I bring a case before you.

Yet I would speak with you about your justice:

Why does the way of the wicked prosper?

Why do all the faithless live at ease? [10]

Elsewhere in the Bible God responds to Jeremiah's anguished question with what amounts to this: "Just hold on. I always balance the books in the end."[11] In the meanwhile, what are we to do? For one thing, we can determine to change our own impatient tendencies and begin to think long term.

PONDERING FUTURE GENERATIONS

Millions of Americans live exclusively in the moment, watching their investments on the Internet or on TV, their eyes glued to the ticker on CNBC. Traders move stocks at breakneck speed; corporate executives hype their IPOs and look for profits robust enough to meet their quarterly goals. All of them create the illusion of wealth for the here and now.

But despite the robber barons of the nineteenth century and the war profiteers, oil tycoons, and dot-com buccaneers of the twentieth, socially responsible wealth rarely gets created in months or years. Usually it takes decades. And such riches should be used to sustain future generations, not to fritter away in sumptuous displays of instant gratification. The Bible says, "A good man leaves an inheritance for his children's children."[12]

I recently shared a meal with a friend from the United Kingdom. He pondered aloud with me the possible state of his family's future. "In fifty years," he said, "my son will be fifty and my grandchild may be twenty. How might I spend my time now so that in that year I can share a journey of beauty and faith with them?"

My friend is contemplating the contours of a life at odds with the dominant culture, an existence filled with the pursuit of things eternal instead of perishable, a life defined by what he can give and not by what he will consume. He is choosing a narrow path, but one that all of us can walk with confidence and peace about where our feet may fall.

The great Iroquois confederation—one of the models for our Founding Fathers as they contemplated our own system of government—believed that in all their council deliberations, they should consider the implications of their actions to the seventh generation. *The seventh generation!* How different from the shortsighted actions pursued by almost all nations, businesses, and individuals today. It would be worthwhile, indeed, if more of us contemplated posterity and the implications of our lives upon future generations.

WHEN IMPATIENCE IS A VIRTUE

Despite what I've said so far, impatience—every now and then—can be a virtue. Consider the response of Dr. Martin Luther King Jr. to certain white Birmingham clergymen who urged him to be patient in his fight for human rights. "It is always the right time to do what is right," he insisted.

Matters of the spirit need tending right away. But when we get in a hurry about gadgets and bank accounts and toys and feasting—things that ultimately matter little when we look back and take stock of our lives—we may be headed for trouble.

Because God's timing is not always our timing, we worry that we must act *now* or lose our piece of the pie. Doesn't our world move on, regardless of our wishes? And news bombards us twenty-four hours a day. We communicate instantaneously with colleagues on far-flung continents. In mere hours we can move our bodies to the four corners of the globe. In such a fast-paced whirlwind of a planet, we worry that if we don't run, we will get swept under the wheels and perish.

But that doesn't have to happen. The wisest among us have always encouraged calm reflection, patient consideration, a faith willing to wait. One Zenlike Psalm speaks of a patient God: "Patience! You've got all the time in the world—whether a thousand years or a day, it's all the same to you."[13]

People of faith do not have to worry overmuch about what might happen should they fail to act quickly enough, for they know that their lives remain continuously in God's hands. "Don't be obsessed with getting more material things," counsels the writer to the Hebrews. "Be relaxed with what you have. Since God assured us, 'I'll never let you down, never walk off and leave you,' we can boldly quote, God is there, ready to help; I'm fearless no matter what. Who or what can get to me?"[14]

And even when bad news and pain pay us an unwelcome visit, they might actually usher in our ultimate happiness. In a poem called "Joy at a Sudden Disappointment," the thirteenth-century Persian mystic poet Rumi wrote,

> Whatever comes, comes from a need,
> a sore distress, a hurting want.
> Mary's pain made the baby Jesus.
> Her womb opened its lips and spoke the Word. . . .
> Be thirsty for the ultimate water,
> and then be ready for what will
> come pouring from the spring.[15]

Why are so many in such a hurry? Why do they insist, as Henry David Thoreau put it, on knowing the things that are never new before they have learned the things that are never old? Why do the biblical commands "Wait for the LORD" and "Be still, and know that I am God," fall on so many deaf ears?[16] Perhaps it can be traced to something no more complicated than a lack of faith. Stanley Hauerwas and William Willimon write:

> The rich are insatiable and can never be content. Having much, they fear the loss of what they have and think the only way to protect what they have is to have more. They thus are tormented and unable to enjoy what they have. Calvin did not need a contemporary psychologist's theory of the "rising threshold of expectation" (the more we have, the more we want) to explain the misery of the miser. Wealth turns into just another name for loneliness. The rich in short just cannot learn to rest easy in God's good creation.[17]

We serve a good God — but too often in our impatience we forget just how good he is. So many things conspire to dim our memories. Life in this world requires tremendous effort. Taking care of our families, and taking care of the world, demands constant work. But Scripture tells us,

> There is far more to your life than the food you put in your stomach, more to your outer appearance than the clothes you hang on your body. Look at the birds, free and unfettered, not tied down to a job description, careless in the care of God. And you count far more to him than birds.[18]

But none of this obliges us to get impatient about making either our marks or our fortunes. Push on toward the prize, the apostle Paul frequently tells us, and you will be rewarded.[19]

So if God should choose to shower riches upon you, bless him. Do a little dance, if you'd like. Then realize why it's been given to you. Not to pamper yourself, but to help the poor. Feed the hungry. Work for justice in the world.

Impatience over things like *this* will keep us from the blunders of Enron.

CHAPTER 11

Sherron Watkins: A Lesson in True Faith

"Has Enron become a risky place to work?"[1]

With that bold question, Sherron Watkins triggered a chain of events that eventually led to the unveiling of the Enron debacle. She wrote her question and hand-delivered it to CEO Ken Lay in August 2001, after she had discovered multiple accounting errors and irregularities among several of the company's transactions that she managed. She continued, "For those of us who didn't get rich over the last few years, can we afford to stay?"[2]

By now, we all know the answers to her respective questions: YES and NO!

FROM ACCOUNTING TO BUSINESS

Watkins, forty-two, the now-famous whistle-blower in one of the largest corporate bankruptcy scandals in history, served as Enron's vice president of corporate development. She earned her bachelor's degree in professional accounting from the University of Texas in 1981 and her master's degree in accounting and business in 1982.

Watkins joined Arthur Andersen in 1982, working first at the company's Houston office, then transferring to New York. She left Arthur Andersen in 1990 and began working for Metallgesellschaft (MG Trade Finance Corporation) in New York. Watkins left Metallgesellschaft in 1993 and went to work in Houston for Andrew Fastow at Enron, managing the company's "$1 billion-plus portfolio of energy related investments held in Enron's various investment vehicles."[3] Watkins joined the company to oversee Fastow's first major Special Purpose Entity account, known as JEDI.

Watkins relocated in 1997 to Enron's international group, focusing primarily on mergers and acquisitions of energy assets around the globe. Then in early 2000, Watkins transferred again into Enron's broadband unit and stayed there until June of 2001, when she returned to work for Fastow. Watkins accepted a new role on Fastow's team to locate company assets that could be sold to bring in more cash and alleviate Enron's debt—the heart of Enron's change from energy company to trading company.

After reviewing Enron's accounts and transactions, Watkins noticed numerous errors in accounting and bookkeeping, which ultimately led her to pen a now-famous seven-page memo to Ken Lay. She expressed her concern: "I am incredibly nervous that we will implode in a wave of accounting scandals."[4]

She was right.

WORLDWIDE RECOGNITION

Although Lay didn't give the issue the attention Watkins thought necessary, her memo has since received worldwide notoriety, serving as a window through which the public might see into the Enron scandal.

Her bravery and honesty in approaching Lay and addressing such colossal issues have earned her much recognition and many awards across the globe. The *London Guardian* hailed Watkins as "the toast of America."[5] Ms. Watkins received the Court TV Scales of Justice Award and its Everyday Hero's Award in May 2002; the Women Mean Business Award from the Business and Professional Women/USA Organization in July 2002; and in January 2002, *Time* magazine named her "Person of the Week" for "putting it in writing and marking the investigative trail."[6]

It has been reported that Watkins dropped by a local Houston Starbucks one morning for coffee, only to be energetically applauded by an approving crowd. Rumors continue to swirl regarding a movie deal "painting [Watkins] as a feminist icon. Some in Hollywood compare her to Erin Brockovich."[7]

Why did so many gravitate to Watkins in the wake of the Enron debacle? Certainly part of it is that Sherron Watkins stood up and said no, even in the face of a "cast-no-doubts" culture at Enron and despite the possibility that she might be putting her job on the line. The *Guardian* remarks,

> Suddenly, the corporate high-flyer was recast as a heroine who stood up to the corrupt, greedy men who had cashed in their shares to make millions of dollars while their deceived employees were trapped in a "stock-lock" which prevented them from doing the same, thereby losing their hard-earned savings and pension funds. On the employees' website— "Laydoff.com" (as in Lay)—Watkins is heralded as "Our Hero" on a T-shirt offered for sale. She gets letters from mothers saying they hold her up as a role model for their teenage daughters.[8]

PEOPLE OF FAITH

Unlike many executives at Enron, Sherron met her eventual spouse at church. In 1997 she married Richard Watkins, also an executive in the energy business. Two years later, Sherron gave birth to their daughter, Marion. The Watkins are people of faith.

When news broke that Sherron had blown the whistle on the sinking ship of Enron, instead of seeking advice from business ethicists, she turned to her pastor and the people in her community. On the day of the press release, Sherron stayed home with her husband. When he told her that camera crews had assembled in their front yard, she first began to shake, then went to her Bible and read from Hebrews 12:

> Therefore, since we are surrounded by such a great cloud of witnesses, let us throw off everything that hinders and the sin that so easily entangles, and let us run with perseverance the race marked out for us. Let us fix our eyes on Jesus, the author and perfecter of our faith, who for the joy set before him endured the cross, scorning its shame, and sat down at the right hand of the throne of God. Consider him who endured such opposition from sinful men, so that you will not grow weary and lose heart.[9]

"This was the perfect passage," Sherron declared. "[It was] God's Word to my heart."[10] That night she attended a dinner at which the speaker quoted the same passage; she took it as divine confirmation.

Sherron Watkins' behavior—her acted-out faith—represents a refreshing change from today's widespread corporate culture of greed and irresponsibility. It has also given hope to people in the business world . . . and in the church. "When our post-Christian culture rejected Christianity," read an essay on the Web site of Friendship Baptist Church in Litchfield, Connecticut,

> it rejected the belief system that makes behavior like Watkins' possible. Today few, if any, business schools teach their students the difference between right and wrong. There are no courses in business ethics, as I discovered when I lectured at Harvard Business School some years ago. So, absent a world-view that thinks in terms of moral absolutes, rather than next quarter's earnings, there's no reason to expect people to act against self-interest and do the right thing. That's why Watkins' actions stand out.[11]

EMBRACING HER LUTHERAN BACKGROUND

In contemplating her role as a "whistle-blower" and in embracing her Lutheran background, Watkins recalls the sixteenth-century German reformer Martin Luther, whom she esteems as one of the first great "whistle-blowers."

Luther was born at Eisleben on November 10, 1483. He went to school at Magdeburg and Eisenach and entered the University of Erfurt in 1501, graduating with a B.A. in 1502 and an M.A. in 1505. His father wanted Martin to be a lawyer, but Martin felt drawn to the study of the Scriptures and spent three years in the Augustinian monastery at Erfurt. In 1507 he was ordained a priest and went to the University of Wittenberg, where he lectured on philosophy and the Scriptures. There, Luther became an authoritative and significant teacher of God's Word.

In July 1505, Luther narrowly escaped electrocution when lightning struck a tree near him, throwing him to the ground. As a result of this brush with death, Luther determined to try to appease God's wrath by becoming a monk. He was ordained into the Augustinian order in 1507.

While visiting Rome in 1510, he felt stunned at the open corruption and wickedness of the officials and clergy of the Roman church. The Germanic churches he knew so well had become separated by both miles and manners from Rome. Luther knew the Scriptures well, and especially in the letters of the apostle Paul he became increasingly aware of the widening gap between what the Roman church taught and biblical standards of truth.

After much study, Luther publicly recognized Christ as the only mediator between God and man and declared that only God's grace could bring salvation. The Roman church could not tolerate his view of redemption, only one of many growing disagreements between the two.

Luther felt especially offended by the sale of indulgences, a form of "Forgiveness for Sale" by the church to ensure sinners remission of sins.

The new archbishop of Mainz had promised to pay the pope a large sum of money—raised by the sale of indulgences—in exchange for his appointment. Luther became livid about this travesty and in response nailed his famous Ninety-Five Theses on the door of Wittenberg Castle Church on October 31, 1517. After trying unsuccessfully to work within the Roman church, Luther blew the whistle on it—and in the process unintentionally started the Protestant Reformation.

Luther wrote, "Whatever man *loves*, that is his god. For he carries it in his *heart*; he goes about with it night and day; he sleeps and wakes with it, be it what it may, wealth or self, pleasure or renown."[12]

The noise Luther made centuries ago continues to echo through time . . . and today hits a bull's-eye in the corporate boardroom.

PICK UP YOUR PEN

Like Luther, Watkins too tried to work within the system. Unlike most top Enron executives, she showed loyalty to both the company and Kenneth Lay. She wrote her first memo to Ken Lay, not to *Nightline.* She believed that Lay still had the power, and perhaps the integrity, to change Enron's course, to correct the wrong.

And even after Lay ignored her warnings and the company began sinking in earnest, she wrote Lay again on October 30, offering her help in unraveling the untruths and in rebuilding the corporation. Her faith gave substance to Luther's admonition almost half a millennium ago, "If you want to change the world, pick up your pen."[13]

Enron's sins, she wrote, had been "horrific," and Enron's fall had occurred through problems "we must all address and fix for corporate America as a whole." With accountability, transparency, and Lay assuming responsibility for what had happened under his watch, Watkins thought the company could still survive.[14]

By now, of course, we know it couldn't and that none of the things she hoped for actually happened. So America got treated to the sight of something highly unusual: an Enron executive willing to testify about the inequities of the system.

Watkins recently said, "My eight years of Enron work history will be worth nothing on my resume. The business world will consider the past successes as nothing but an elaborate accounting hoax."[15]

Still, it is to be hoped that all of us will remember Sherron Watkins as an example of integrity in a time and place where no one willingly spoke truth to power—or even spoke at all.

CHAPTER 12

The Fatal Flaw of the Western World

I recently had dinner with a former Enron VP. "I'd love to tell you the whole story," he declared, "but I need to know what's in it for me."

"This isn't a tell-all book," I replied, "and what you just told me will illustrate my point quite nicely."

What's in it for me? You can almost hear the accountants chanting the words when asked yet again to stretch the boundaries of ethics and common decency. It seems, many at the top levels of Enron shared a grandiose piece of stockholder pie by leaving the workingman to pay the tab. Workers dismantling Enron's London office, for example, found the following luxury items:

- an electric train set used to deliver bonuses to high-performing executives
- a high-tech gym
- a ToneZone for aromatherapy, tanning, and beauty treatments
- pricey paintings and sculptures
- a thirty-three-foot maple veneer conference table inlaid with solid walnut
- marble-covered garbage bins[1]

Recent revelations about similar opulent perks for the CEOs and top executives of other companies have made notorious a similar kind of widespread depredation. So, is capitalism to blame for this *Fortune 500* fallout? Has our economic system caused the nation's current corporate crisis?

In a word, no.

AN UNHOLY MARRIAGE

Our free-market system honors those who work hard and gives force to the biblical principle that "if a man will not work, he shall not eat."[2] We Americans have pursued material success since our beginnings, when the Puritans of the Massachusetts Bay Colony considered wealth a sign of God's election and helped to create our culture of commodity.

When capitalism unwittingly marries unbridled Western individualism, however, catastrophe results. In such a system, every person creates a society for himself or herself, thus making a mockery of the idea of a nation of liberty and freedom.

The thinking behind such a warped worldview goes something like this: *If in my freedom I make choices based solely on profit—even if those choices devastate the lives of hundreds or even thousands of people—I shouldn't feel guilty. It's my right, and it's the American way.*

How fitting, then, that the now-famous "Crooked E" outside of Enron's headquarters (one such sign recently netted $40,000 at auction) stood alongside the American flag. Why fitting? Because the Tao of Enron reflects an American brand of individualism gone badly wrong.

HOLLOW WORDS, USELESS CODES

Enron made a point of creating and promoting "core values" (respect, integrity, communication, excellence) with which every employee was supposed to become familiar. These values, if followed, would have created a very different Enron.

But as former Enron employee Brian Cruver points out, "Rarely has the difference between sermon and conduct been so dramatic. The contrast between Enron's moral mantra and the behavior of some Enron executives is bone-chilling. Indeed, the Enron saga teaches us the limitations of corporate codes of ethics. . . . Codes are useless when the words are hollow."[3]

An outsider looking at the Enron collapse might describe many of its executives in the words of the prophet Isaiah, who pictured the leaders of his generation as voracious dogs with never enough to eat: "They know nothing, understand nothing. They all look after themselves, grabbing whatever's not nailed down."[4]

Of course, the Creator of heaven and earth had something very different in mind for his creation. The Bible tells us to approach life and finances with an open hand, offering "your surplus matching their deficit, their surplus matching your deficit. In the end you come out even."[5]

Until we Americans re-envision the role of business and wealth, we are doomed to repeat a series of disasters like what happened at Enron. And the fallout for most of us will not come in the form of the collapse of the seventh largest company in the United States of America; it will take shape in the collapse of marriages, families, and communities, and the suffering of children and other helpless victims across the planet—all because of our selfish choices.

The time has come for a new worldview, a new way of seeing that puts "we" before "me."

EAST AND WEST

After September 11, many Americans began to wake up to the vast difference in worldviews between the East and West. Middle Easterners have dubbed Western nations "the great Satan" at least in part as a result of a brutal history of violence and persecution, including religious wars immortalized in the West as "the Crusades."

Decades of worldwide "Coca-Colonization"—the aggressive spread of American business into foreign markets—and a history of American intervention in the Middle East, often on behalf of those corporations, has left many in that area of the world with intense feelings of hatred and resentment toward us.

Such a turn of events surprises many among us and causes us to react with indignation. "But I did not do anything to cause you harm!" we protest. And from our point of view, we speak the truth. In all likelihood we did not personally take up a gun or a fountain pen to rape the Third World; probably we did not personally participate in the CIA coup in Iran in the 1950s. In the West, "I" means "me"—but not in the East.

In the East, "I" means "we." That part of the world does not so easily forget historical and generational sins. In the eyes of most Middle Easterners, we Americans stand guilty of a number of sins against their countries and people.

Most of us in the Land of Plenty find such an idea hard to fathom. After all, we live in a nation ravaged less than a century and a half ago by a vicious civil war—yet today the conflict seems all but forgotten. The fierce grudges and open hostility generated by the war have almost entirely died out (except, perhaps, for a few backwater hamlets in the deep South). The conflicts that led to the Civil War were "their" conflicts, not ours.

Or consider the dilemma of race relations. Polls show that most white Americans dismiss racism as a bogeyman of the past. They think of it as an issue only for a few deranged individuals — a handful of illiterate, hate-filled rednecks who shave their misshapen heads when they're not covering them with pointy white hoods or ducking into secluded bunkers. And so we say things like, "If I can make it to the top, why can't anyone else?"

Christianity Today recently quoted a Presbyterian man as declaring, "I think our country has a perceived race relations problem. I think that we have individuals still that have race relation problems. I don't think that the country has in its current form a race relation problem."[6]

Yet despite such a rose-colored perspective, racism continues to plague this nation — just ask any African American. Why does it persist? One reason racism persists is because our commitment to radical individualism allows us to discount the continuing reality of racial discrimination. In other words, we think "me" instead of "we."

But the hatred of even a few injures us all and reveals a deadly sickness afflicting our entire society. Our willingness to set racial issues aside before completely solving them provides a sad measure of our willing blindness. Martin Luther King Jr. famously argued that injustice anywhere is a threat to justice everywhere. If any of us suffer from prejudice and discrimination, then we all have a problem.

We dare not forget that we stand only a half-century removed from an American South that celebrated prejudice with public lynchings. Even today, racial injustice persists in our nation, and not only in the South. Graphic accounts of the Los Angeles police beating of

Rodney King and the New York police shooting of the unarmed Abner Diallo stand morbidly alongside the East-Texas lynching of James Byrd Jr.

How can we identify with human oppression in North Korea and slavery in the Sudan if we cannot stand up for the man who lives in our own city? If we cannot see our next-door neighbors as brothers, then the family in the Philippines and the widow in Cuba will never elicit our sympathy or compassion.

The Western view (being-as-self) and that of its Eastern counterparts (being-as-community) stand in total contradiction to one another. While citizens of the West embrace a spiritual and philosophical tradition of individualism, our Eastern counterparts approach the world with a communal view that considers their existence as part of the greater whole. They see everything and everyone as interconnected.

Once, when I asked a friend from mainland China about American individualism, he told me quite plainly, "I could never separate myself from my family and my people. I am a part of them, and they are a part of me." This is not blind loyalty; rather, it is a profound understanding of self—one that could benefit us tremendously.

THE PLAGUE OF SELF-ACTUALIZATION

Instead of seeking the benefit of all, we have come to believe that only by being free to act as individuals can we truly be ourselves.

Our nation has embraced the bankrupt philosophy of Abraham Maslow, who taught that the ultimate state of being is self-actualization, a kind of nirvana where all of our so-called needs get met. Happiness, pleasure, and emotional contentment become needs by definition, something we *must* have. Such a philosophy of life seeks to feed the desires of the individual above all else—and yet experience tells us that those who make happiness their primary goal rarely find it.

The frantic pursuit of self-actualization provides one powerful reason for the endemic despair and depression that plagues our culture. We can never eat enough, get enough, have sex enough, or shoot up enough to fill the empty place inside ourselves (although plenty of people die trying).

The sexual escapades of many Enron executives—divorcing wives to marry secretaries, traveling with "harems" of secretaries and female assistants—provide yet another example of our society's firm commitment to satisfying self above all. According to Robert Bryce, "The Enron story has no peers when it comes to high-level sexual shenanigans. . . . There were several quite public affairs, and it became a self-fulfilling presumption: 'Neither the sexual rules nor the financial rules apply to us, because we're smarter, faster, and better-looking than anyone else in town.'"[7] Such lurid stories indict our culture more powerfully than any corporate bankruptcy ever could.

American men in search of self-actualization often betray their own families and lead them down a road of destruction and separation. Seeking to gratify the self, they become infatuated with younger, more vivacious women—or they simply get bored. And then the real trouble begins.

Because we covet great wealth, our society tends to honor without question the thieves who take whatever they want. Stanley Hauerwas reminds us of a powerful truth taught by an earlier reformer who spoke of commercial fraud:

> Calvin observes that this crime is made worse because often
> the thief is applauded. Indeed he is not just applauded, but

honored because he is such a big thief. For, as a man's estate
grows, people woo him and he becomes more admired.
Therefore, as far as the world is concerned, quite often it is
through theft that people are honored.[8]

When we make gratifying the self our goal, then the one who best
manages to coddle himself or herself gets named the winner and
receives the praise and accolades due the victor. But what a hollow
victory it is.

LOSS OF COMMUNITY

Technological advancement, and the affluence that usually comes
with it, puts community on the back burner and allows us to function independently of one another. We have our own cars, our own
swimming pools, our own playgrounds. We order over the Internet
instead of making human contact in a local store. We become
autonomous.

Many of us have used our affluence to allow us to function without community and even without family. Enron illustrates both how
financial excess tends to destroy community and how loss of community injures people.

Many of Enron's failures sprang from feelings of isolation, a lack
of brotherhood, and the devaluation of accountability. Robert Bryce
suggests that this was in fact the chief reason Enron imploded: "There
was no esprit de corps, no co-responsibility, for anyone else in the
company or for the company as a whole, or any sense of a larger, common community of interest."[9] Executives built parts of Enron on the
philosophy that it made sense to overpay young, inexperienced MBAs
at the expense of older employees. Why did it make sense? Because

those older employees usually had grown too set in their ways to appreciate the independence and lack of accountability necessary to enable bright young stars to spend whatever they deemed prudent in pursuit of new business opportunities.

Representatives of the companies Jeff Skilling built gave a common recruiting response to those who might have felt some connection to a wife and perhaps children. Those who asked about time with family received a twofold response: (1) We pay so much more than you can make anywhere else that you'll be able to afford great vacations; and (2) If you expect more family time, go visit some of our competitors.

Stanley Hauerwas, professor of Christian ethics and law at Duke Divinity School, has made some potent observations about poverty, wealth, and the effect of affluence on community:

> I think that what God is doing is teaching us that
> Christianity is very much about knowing how to go on in the
> face of being poor. I don't want at all to romanticize poverty,
> but the poor are forced into forms of cooperation that pro-
> vide resources that we affluent Christians do not have. It takes
> a lot of money to avoid cooperating with other people.
> Affluent Western Christians have that kind of money.[10]

Author John McKnight explores the connection between wealth and the loss of kinship in his book *The Careless Community*, demonstrating how modern systems made possible by wealth have radically changed the face of America and the way we relate to one another.

I contemplated McKnight's thesis during a recent trip to Philadelphia. I relished my place on the train, a modern convenience with the power to carry me to my destination. That summer, the bus drivers in Philly had gone on strike and many of my fellow passengers had to walk miles to the train line to get to and from work. As I sat alone in my seat, reading and thinking, I tried to imagine life without mass urban-transit systems. I managed almost that whole trip (like many others) without actually speaking to another living soul. Throughout most of my journey I remained disconnected, autonomous, and selfish—and didn't even know it.

That is, until our train stopped dead in its tracks. The striking bus drivers had somehow managed to stop the trains to strengthen their bargaining position. For more than two hours our train sat still in a dark tunnel.

Only then did I witness a hint of real community.

When modern systems collapse, we are forced to come together. Our experience on the motionless train felt to me like the church in Acts where they "shared everything they had."[11] Over the course of two hours we shared what little food we possessed, laughed, and told stories about our life and families. We created a communal meal out of an apple, crackers, cheese, and a few packs of gum. One gentleman had a cell phone and let almost forty people use it to inform their families that they would be late. For more than 120 minutes we enjoyed real community—but most days we get by without ever acknowledging those around us. Why? Because we don't need them.

We sit in our own cars, cook in our own kitchens, and can hunker down in the bunkers of our own homes. Yet our isolation destroys us from the inside. We are made in the image of God as relational beings, and we cannot heal our lack of connectedness through increased profits, Prozac, or psychotherapy. "It is not good for the man to be alone,"[12] God said at the beginning of human history, and his diagnosis remains unchanged. Our lust for more and bigger and

newer, however, relentlessly pushes us away from others and into isolated settings, where we find ourselves very much alone. In the end,
the "woe" of Isaiah the prophet comes crashing into our eardrums:

> Woe to you who add house to house
> > and join field to field
> till no space is left
> > and you live alone in the land.[13]

WHAT'S THE ANSWER?

More than one reader might recommend that greedy betrayers should
go to church—but many of the traitors of the Enron Corp. describe
themselves as people of faith.

Is this, then, an indictment of organized religion? And if not, is
there *some* way to ensure that people will not corrupt themselves?
Perhaps we could all just follow a common code of ethics, such as the
Ten Commandments, or even the Golden Rule. Could we then cease
worshiping money?

History, personal experience, and Scripture all agree that the rule
of law *cannot* eliminate the type of greed and criminal misconduct
that allows people, like some top executives at Enron, to swim in luxury at the expense of thousands robbed of their jobs, homes, financial
security, and medical care.

Americans enjoy the autonomy of radical individualism, but it
comes at a terrible cost. We must make a choice; it is impossible to have
both autonomy and vigorous health. If we want the latter, we have no
choice but to embrace community over radical individualism. In doing
so—in gaining a strong sense of "we"—we actually strengthen the "I."
The two do not oppose, but complement, one another.

In accepting the 1984 Nobel Peace Prize, Archbishop Desmond Tutu said, "God created us for fellowship. God created us so that we should form the human family, existing together because we were made for each other. We are not made for an exclusive self-sufficiency but for interdependence, and we break that law of being at our peril."[14]

It is possible to become strong, vibrant men and women who live with a strong awareness of communal obligations. Living such a life will strengthen, not weaken, our businesses, neighborhoods, families, churches, and the environment. Our commitment will ring out into the world and resound throughout its distant four corners like the loud peal of a village bell.

Ultimately, an *individual* finds integrated integrity, honor, and usefulness only in relation to his or her *community*. A finger remains honored and useful only so long as it stays attached to the hand. When we separate ourselves from the body, from our community, we lose both our honor and our usefulness.

So once again: how do we reject radical individualism and instead embrace a commitment to community? Do we make new laws? Write new constitutions? Frame better ordinances? While some of that might help, it won't help much. Our problems will not be fixed by a new president, nor by a vigilant Securities and Exchange Commission, nor by a slew of legislation designed to infuse morality and decency into a population bubbling over with selfishness, escapism, and greed.

Only a change of heart can do that.

A NOBLE CAUSE

We are a diverse people, and a healthy commitment to community will not come through forced conformity or artificial homogeneity. So how do we create a sense of community in a nation of individuals?

After September 11, our nation came together to fight a common enemy; but hatred and a desire for revenge can never create lasting community. Throughout our history, the cold war and other wars have tended to crystallize into conflicts of "us" against "them." Our challenge is to define an "us" not in terms of who we are *not*, but who we *are*.

We foster true brotherhood and create healthy community when we share life's experiences and join one another in a common mission. We can learn from bright, selfless moments of our past, such as:

• the civil rights movement
• the drive for public education
• the rural electrification initiative
• the environmental movement

More than anything, we need a noble cause to unify us. Where can we find it? I maintain that we discover a worthy purpose when we commit ourselves to service and generosity in order to remedy the enormous problems of poverty, homelessness, illness, and disease. It is time to confess our obsession with self-aggrandizement and accept the responsibility of helping our brothers and sisters who join us on this journey.

Are we there yet? Not by a long shot. In fact, one might describe our current state with some stinging words from Scripture: "Most people around here are looking out for themselves, with little concern for the things of Jesus."[15]

But we need not—must not—remain in this state. The "things of Jesus" include caring for the poor, widows, and the helpless. If we join together in tackling these daunting tasks, we will find ourselves becoming a better people. And if we join together to serve others, we will discover how a living faith can change the world for the better.

We find real joy when we get outside of ourselves and seek the good of others before our own. In fact, the ability to lose one's self in a greater good is one of the great beauties of the Christian life. A God who "made himself nothing" for our own good calls on each of us to do the same.[16]

CHAPTER 13

J. Clifford Baxter: Life Is Fleeting

Friends knew Cliff Baxter as a family man, a generous benefactor, and a brilliant deal maker. His story reminds us of the beauty of life and the painful sting of death. Consider him the most tragic character in the Enron play.

DEATH IN BLOCK LETTERS

They found the note, written in block letters and addressed to his wife, in an envelope just next to Cliff Baxter's body. It read:

> CAROL,
> I AM SO SORRY FOR THIS. I FEEL I JUST CAN'T GO
> ON. I HAVE ALWAYS TRIED TO DO THE RIGHT THING BUT
> WHERE THERE WAS ONCE GREAT PRIDE NOW IT'S GONE.
> I LOVE YOU AND THE CHILDREN SO MUCH. I JUST CAN'T
> BE ANY GOOD TO YOU OR MYSELF. THE PAIN IS OVER-
> WHELMING. PLEASE TRY TO FORGIVE ME.
> CLIFF

Officials found the note and the body on January 25, 2002, in Clifford Baxter's brand new 2002 Mercedes Benz, not far from his suburban Houston home in Sugar Land, Texas. The letter seemingly sealed the case for local authorities: a suicide. Local Justice of the Peace Jim Richards declared the cause of death to be a self-inflicted gunshot wound to the head.

Many observers, however, remain unsatisfied with that verdict and believe this note gives evidence not only of Baxter's tragic demise at age forty-three, but also, perhaps, of a more sinister cause of death.

In his article "The Strange and Convenient Death of J. Clifford Baxter — Enron Executive Found Shot to Death," Patrick Martin writes,

> The circumstances of Baxter's life cast doubt on the verdict of suicide. He is not known to have been suffering from depression or any other mental health problem. He was a multimillionaire, having netted $30 million from the sale of his stock in the company before and after his departure from Enron [in May 2001]. His family life was apparently happy, and he leaves a wife and two children, a 16-year-old son and 11-year-old daughter. Far from being the target of media vilification, Baxter's name had been linked to the Enron affair in a way that was largely favorable.[1]

An executive of Portland Gas & Electric, an Enron subsidiary whose $3 billion acquisition Baxter had negotiated, told the *New York Times*, "My impression of Cliff Baxter was that this was an enormously confident guy who came up here to get the thing done, and he did. The image I had of him at the time is totally at odds with the tragedy today. I mean, he was self-assured; he was very friendly. This was practically the last person in the world you'd ever expect to commit suicide."[2]

Which is why, perhaps, some people still suspect that he didn't.

A DISTINGUISHED CAREER MAN

Baxter was born in Amityville, New York, on September 27, 1958. After attending New York University, he joined the U.S. Air Force, where he enjoyed a distinguished career as an officer.

After his stint in the military, Baxter received an M.B.A. in business administration from Columbia Business School in 1987 and worked as an investment banker before joining Enron in 1990. Baxter helped transform Enron from a simple pipeline company into a global energy trader. He served as chairman and chief executive of Enron North America before he became its chief strategy officer, and then vice chairman in October 2000. Baxter resigned as vice chairman of the company in May 2001 to spend more time with his family: his wife of nineteen years, Carol; his sixteen-year-old son, J. C.; and his eleven-year-old daughter, Lauren Elizabeth.

Seven years before turning fifty, Baxter had joined a select club of retired millionaires. He had made a profit of $21,980,470 from selling nearly six hundred thousand shares of Enron, owned a mansion in an affluent suburb of Houston, and had purchased a yacht.

Baxter had earned a good reputation in the community for his support of charitable organizations and endeavors. He had formerly served on the board of Junior Achievement of the Houston Gulf Coast and of Houston's Epilepsy Association. His vast wealth had enabled him to leave behind a seemingly successful career at the energy giant for a life in which he could pursue his passion — boating — and enjoy spending time with his family. His life seemed to have begun again.

And then, without warning, it ended.

THE RESPECT OF PEERS

Of all the players in the Enron debacle, it seems Clifford Baxter generated the most evenhanded response. BBC News described Baxter as "a living embodiment of the American dream."[3] He seemed to have everything—a great job, a beautiful family, the genuine respect of his peers and employees.

In that BBC story, Kevin Hyatt, Enron's director of pipeline business development, remembered Baxter as "one of the best mentors I've had. . . . He was ruthless when it came to working a deal. Definitely a guy you wanted on your side and not against you. . . . But when it came to people around him, people who worked for him, he genuinely cared . . . about the employees and their families."[4]

Philip Hilder, Sherron Watkins' attorney, said that Watkins was "deeply saddened and stunned beyond belief" by Baxter's death. "Mr. Baxter had the utmost integrity and she respected him immensely. Mrs. Watkins expresses her heartfelt sympathy and prayers to his family," said Hilder.[5]

At the time of Baxter's resignation, Jeff Skilling, then Enron's CEO, said, "Over the past ten years, Cliff has made a tremendous contribution to Enron's evolution, particularly as a member of the team that built Enron's wholesale business. His creativity, intelligence, sense of humor, and straightforward manner have been assets to the company throughout his career."[6] Certainly they had—and his departure troubled many within Enron who thought of him as "the conscience of the company."[7]

So why would a man seen to embody the integrity often lacking at Enron *kill* himself? This remains an unanswered question. Of all the things that might be said or argued about Clifford Baxter's death, however, one thing seems clear: boardroom deception can generate fatal consequences. No one could have imagined that the greed birthed at the downtown headquarters of Enron Corp. would eventually give birth to death on the streets of an exclusive, gated community. Regardless of the manner of Clifford Baxter's death, Enron destroyed the man just as surely as if the corporate tower had toppled on him.

WHAT LIES AHEAD?

No one knows what lies ahead for any of us — and we never have. Therefore an ancient song master could declare to his heavenly Lord, "Remember how fleeting is my life. For what futility you have created all men!"[8]

In a similar way, Israel's celebrated King David contemplated his future fate with a wise prayer:

> Show me, O LORD, my life's end
> and the number of my days;
> let me know how fleeting is my life.
> You have made my days a mere handbreadth;
> the span of my years is as nothing before you.
> Each man's life is but a breath.
> Man is a mere phantom as he goes to and fro:
> He bustles about, but only in vain;
> he heaps up wealth, not knowing who will get it.[9]

In the end, does it matter even a little how much wealth you manage to pile up? Of course not. It can all be taken away in a moment. And when that moment comes, whether you're seated in a luxury Mercedes-Benz or a rusted-out Hyundai, your part in the drama has ended.

And there will be no encores.

CHAPTER 14

Chris Bryan: Willing to Walk Away

It seems that a growing majority of Americans, faced with the choice of either stifling their Christian convictions or walking away from a high-paying job, end up opting for the cash. But not everyone makes such a decision.

As one example, meet Chris Bryan.

A CAREER IN ENERGY

Chris Bryan graduated from Texas Tech in Lubbock in 1969 with a BBA in personnel management. He began working in the energy industry thirty-two years ago, at the age of twenty-two, as an industrial relations representative for Texaco in Houston. He later transferred from Houston to Coral Gables, Florida, and then to Quito, Ecuador, where a local missionary baptized him in response to his profession of faith in Christ.

Bryan left Texaco in 1974 and moved to Aramco Services Company. His wife, Judy—the couple has been married now for nearly thirty years—gave birth to their first daughter, Heather, in

1975, and to Amy Pogue, their second, in 1976. In time Bryan left Aramco to join Roy M. Huffington, Inc., then went to Natomas, until he transferred again in December of 1984 to Houston Natural Gas (later turned Enron) as VP of Employee Relations. Following the merger with Internorth, he was assigned to Enron's exploration and production company as VP of Administration and Human Resources.

Bryan traveled extensively on work assignments, from Ecuador to Saudi Arabia to Indonesia to India to Trinidad and Tobago to Venezuela to Russia to China. But eventually he came to notice how his division (Enron Oil and Gas) operated in ways significantly different from that of its majority shareholder (Enron).

It takes a lot of capital to explore for oil and gas and to develop production capabilities. Forrest Hoglund, chairman of Enron Oil and Gas, "never let up on keeping overhead costs down to free up more money for drilling wells," Bryan said. "He made good businesspeople out of all his managers through the quarterly review process. Forrest and his small group of headquarters function-heads personally visited each division office every three months to compare results with what had been presented and approved during the previous review."

In fact, virtually every geologist, geophysicist, landman, and engineer under Hoglund's supervision had the opportunity every three months to present her or his work to the chairman. In turn, the chairman saw the work product and knew the results achieved by every technical employee in his decentralized company. He also "insisted on being made aware of every planned expenditure," Bryan said, "and spent more time making sure the financial numbers made sense than he did in reviewing all the details of expensive acquisitions or wildcat wells."

According to Bryan, Hoglund was no "hands-off" leader who left operating procedures up to the whims of managers. He knew exactly what was happening in his company—and everyone counted on the fact.

"Hoglund was serious about how his company operated," Bryan said. "He knew the business so well that even the brightest people learned they could not misrepresent technical or financial data without getting nailed. Because of his leadership, what he built still survives as the profitable EOG Resources. He and his outside board members managed to keep Skilling and Baxter and others from destroying his company's ability to remain profitable."

TIME TO LEAVE

As Bryan increasingly began to notice how things that opposed his faith routinely received encouragement and praise at the parent company, he started to give serious thought to leaving Enron. Consider just two examples of the kind of troubling incidents that gave him pause.

One day senior human resources managers with compensation responsibilities met to ensure "some semblance of coordination of merit spending and bonus pools," Bryan said. "I remarked that corporate executives appeared to be getting out of line, on the high side. One of the corporate compensation people suggested that I shut up and get in line. I thought at first that he wanted only to break for lunch—that was, until I saw what the Enron board of directors eventually approved."

Another time, during the last corporate-wide human resources conference that Bryan attended, the newly recruited corporate VP with responsibilities for marketing the Enron name rolled out a campaign to hype the company's vision and values. She envisioned banners hanging in the lobby and a multitude of other marketing gimmicks to loudly proclaim what Enron supposedly stood for. "Yet we were very little of what the glitzy campaign was going to promote," Bryan said. "I boiled as the 'show' continued. When it was finally over and the HR community of around three hundred were polled for reactions, I told them that while we could say these things represented what we would *strive* to become, we could not say we *are* to any of it. Aside from a few people who agreed out loud—and most of them were from Portland—the majority neither appreciated nor wanted to hear my remarks. In my mind, telling prospective employees—those being recruited off campus and especially those who already had good jobs elsewhere—that Enron was what this campaign described, lacked both truth and integrity. It amounted to lying to people about what they could expect if they turned down other offers of employment or left their current employer."

But Chris Bryan left the company also because of a spiritual turbulence growing inside of *himself*. "I had been struggling for years with why more Christians, including myself, didn't truly live their lives as though they believed that God is who the Bible says he is," he said. "Except for attending church on a regular basis, very few Christians seemed much different from other people. In fact, I worked with nonChristians who behaved much better than some who had Bibles visible in their offices, Bibles that contained verses like: 'Seek ye first the kingdom of God'; 'Love the Lord thy God with all thy heart, and with all thy soul, and with all thy mind'; 'A double minded man is unstable in all his ways'; and 'No one can serve two masters.'[1] All those verses kept coming into my mind. I believed they were true; but what did they require of *me*?"

Chris says that remorse over the amount of time he spent on the job and away from his family seemed to grow within him as his youngest daughter married and then his father became ill and slowly died.

"I realized I had not taken time to enjoy my daughters," he confessed, "and I wondered, as my dad lay sick in his bed for over six months, what he was thinking. My mother did everything but breathe for him. What thoughts ruled his mind? What regrets did he have? What opportunities had he missed? Did he look forward to death, and if so, for what reasons? Right up to the end he didn't need any pain medication and he never lost his sense of humor or his ability to express his love for us, especially his granddaughters. So I determined that when it came my time to go, I also would be able to leave without regret."

As Chris read a few Christian classics and pondered his situation, a new conviction began to grow. C. S. Lewis' book *Mere Christianity* "crystallized much of my skepticism about my own behavior and constant struggle with God's involvement with his creation," he said. "I'll always remember one funny statement that changed my life: 'You can't just go on being a good egg. You either have to hatch or rot.' I didn't know the shelf life of an egg, but I couldn't wait to get into an incubator."

He finally took the plunge and resigned his position in July 1997.

"Making the *decision* to leave Enron Oil and Gas was the not hard part," he said. "*Leaving* was. It seemed selfish and certainly self-centered, especially since I did not have what many term as a clear 'calling' from God to do anything else. I knew there were major financial consequences associated with leaving a great job. But because we had always lived well under our income, we still had plenty."

MOVING TO MINISTRY

After leaving Enron, Bryan studied theology and ministry at Baylor University's Truett Seminary, graduating in 2000 with a master of divinity degree. "I knew I wanted to complete seminary," Chris admits, "because I still had too many questions I needed to answer for myself."

While at seminary, Chris's finances seemed secure and growing—he had left his retirement savings in Enron stock on the pronouncements of a Wall Street analyst who said, "If there is one stock everybody should own, it's Enron"—but things took a turn for the worse after graduation.

"When I completed Truett, our net worth was greater than when we began," he said, "even though neither of us received a paycheck for two and a half years. It was all due to the appreciation of my Enron stock. Now, at two and a half years after graduation, we are both working and have lost more than 60 percent of what we once had."

So does he regret his decision? Not for a moment, says he. He finds ministry more compelling than anything he ever accomplished in the energy industry.

In August 2000, Bryan accepted a position as associate pastor at Baptist Temple Church in Houston. Then, in 2002, he began working as interim administrator at Baptist Mission Centers. In the future he plans to serve as a part-time chaplain with MarketPlace Ministries.

WHICH COST DO YOU CHOOSE?

Can a Christian who wants to honor God with his or her whole life continue to work for a corporation that routinely extols and promotes business practices anathema to a strong biblical faith? For Chris Bryan, the answer was no.

Did his decision cost him? Without question. But for Bryan, the real question was, what would it have cost him *not* to make his decision?

And despite how the Enron fallout hurt him personally, Bryan still has hope that at least some of those involved in the fiasco will one day wake up and open their spiritual eyes.

"It is my prayer that wealthy people from Vinson and Elkins, Arthur Andersen, Wall Street, business schools, Citibank, Morgan Stanley, and McKinsey will join with members of the old Enron board of directors—Ken Lay, Jeff Skilling, Rebecca Mark, Andy Fastow, Rick Causey, and others—and study Luke 19:1-9."

An assignment that no doubt would benefit us all.

CHAPTER 15

On Trial in the Court of the Creator

Television pundits and armchair executives daily ponder what's in store for the embattled former corporate executives of Enron. CNN's *Moneyline* broadcasts the daily scoreboard of high-profile executives newly facing indictment.

America is calling for blood. Someone has to pay.

Even in days of old, when society deemed as fair the principle of "an eye for an eye," justice would be difficult to find in such a mess. The business leaders in question appear to have taken more than they could ever repay. The fiasco involves more than the loss of monetary riches, corporate respectability, and shareholder confidence. Some have lost their lives and many families have suffered devastatng losses. Justice seems elusive, a chasing after the wind.

Fear reigns in the lives of powerful men and women once seen as the best and brightest executives in the world. These individuals wake up each morning only to be served with another lawsuit. They desperately clutch to their breasts the homes, cars, and art that appear to be slipping away from them.

Crime, be it blue or white collar, does not pay. Money cannot fill the black vacuum of emptiness and isolation. The constant threat of prosecution and the hot breath of federal investigators breathing down perspiring necks make impossible a life of ease, or even of sound sleep.

Meanwhile, former employees are taking matters into their own hands. They're flooding civil courts with lawsuits, attempting to hold their former bosses accountable for their financial losses. Angry people demand restitution.

Of course, some wealth will be redistributed, mostly to trial lawyers and a small minority of employees and shareholders. But will what is truly just and right be accomplished on this earth? No.

Nevertheless, these executives *will* be held accountable to a higher court—and so will we.

TURNING THE TABLES

Even as we relish the idea that the guilty will get their just deserts, we ought to remember that we will also get ours. Nearly two millennia ago Jesus witnessed a bloodthirsty mob—not unlike the current group of federal prosecutors and former stockholders and employees—pursuing a woman caught in adultery. They wanted her dead.

As they gathered stones to pummel the accused into the great beyond, Christ turned the tables. "If any one of you is without sin, let him be the first to throw a stone at her," he said calmly.[1] Moments before, self-righteousness had spewed out of each smug face as the sputtering men focused on the vile nature of this woman. But when the accusations unexpectedly got turned their way, they had to face their own sullied nature: Depraved. Selfish. Sinful.

And the accusers now stood accused.

Jamie Wells, visual arts pastor at Ecclesia, tells this famous story in her own way through a four-by-four-foot canvas that hangs boldly in her home gallery. She created the piece after a Dallas church commissioned her to paint it. But when the church saw the narrative she brought to life so unashamedly, it refused to pay.

The image portrays a woman, nude, lying facedown and sprawled on top of a covert cross with an unknown man whispering the words, "Go and sin no more." Above the naked woman stands another person—the same woman, spiritlike—walking away, newly dressed in white, a beautiful picture of grace and forgiveness.

The story speaks to us all.

With great ease we pile judgment onto Ken Lay and his cohorts, never realizing that we are cut from the same fabric. No one on this earth lives free of pride, greed, and selfishness.

Can you imagine being the object of so much hatred? Some call Ken Lay the most hated man in America. As the public—including federal prosecutors, television personalities, politicians, and newspaper columnists—stir one another into a vengeful frenzy, you can almost hear the gentle words of the Messiah turning the tables on his would-be executioners. To them he says, "Let the one with no sin throw the first stone." And to the guilty, "Go now and leave your life of sin."[2] In doing so, Jesus has turned the tables on us all and exposed our own bankrupt values and selfish schemes.

BEFORE THE BAR

We all stand accused and the little book of Micah speaks of our prosecution. The prophet tells us that all of God's people have become defendants in the courtroom of the creator. God has charged us all with the same kind of greed, selfishness, and evil plotting that doomed Enron.

The star witness? You might be surprised. No chance here of bribing the speaker or of influencing his testimony. For the one taking the stand against us is none other than the Lord God Almighty, creator of heaven and earth.

So it is clear from the start: we don't stand a chance. God sits in the witness chair to offer his untarnished testimony as proof of our dark motives. And no longer can we sit in judgment over Skilling, Fastow, Mark, and Lay.

Now *we* are on trial.

All of us who pollute the air, horde wealth at the expense of others — "others" being, in our era, predominantly children — and take what we want without regard for the rest of God's creation have been called to give an account. God has had enough and is calling out, "Don't you know anything of justice? Haters of good, lovers of evil: Isn't justice in your job description? But you skin my people alive. You rip the meat off their bones. You break up the bones, chop the meat, and throw it in a pot for cannibal stew."[3]

Corporate culture in America has resorted to savagery. Discontent with our levels of wealth, we have resorted to cannibalism. We have taken consumption to a strange conclusion: a feast on the flesh of our fellow citizens.

If God chose to personally address the Enron fallout, I believe he might take out a full-page ad in the *Wall Street Journal* and announce his displeasure with some startling words from his servant, Micah:

Attention! GOD calls out to the city!
If you know what's good for you, you'll listen.

So listen, all of you!

    This is serious business.

"Do you expect me to overlook obscene wealth

    you've piled up by cheating and fraud?

Do you think I'll tolerate shady deals

    and shifty scheming?

I'm tired of the violent rich

    bullying their way with bluffs and lies.

I'm fed up. Beginning now, you're finished.

    You'll pay for your sins down to your last cent.

No matter how much you get, it will never be enough—

    hollow stomachs, empty hearts.

No matter how hard you work, you'll have nothing to show
for it—

    bankrupt lives, wasted souls.

You'll plant grass

    but never get a lawn.

You'll make jelly

    but never spread it on your bread.

You'll press apples

    but never drink the cider.

You have lived by the standards of your king, Omri,

    the decadent lifestyle of the family of Ahab.

Because you've slavishly followed their fashions,

    I'm forcing you into bankruptcy."[4]

Think this harsh indictment pertains only to some ancient criminals? Think again. Heaven's prosecutor has built a strong case against us:

- A "State of the World's Children" report, issued by UNICEF on December 16, 1997, states that malnutrition contributes to nearly seven million child deaths every year—more than any infectious disease, war, or natural disaster.[5]

- Some 800,000 to 900,000 people in the United States are HIV-positive. More than 300,000 people live with AIDS. Each year, about 40,000 new infections occur.[6] And the numbers soar when you consider the worldwide AIDS epidemic.

- Sixteen million orphans around the world have been created through AIDS, war, exploding landmines, poverty, and famine. Studies and news reports indicate that this number is expected to triple in the next few years. "Life for these parentless children is desperate. They are forced to beg for food. They are often the victims of sexual predators and violent assaults because there are no adults left to care for them."[7] Many who have traveled in countries such as India and Indonesia have seen children who as babies were purposely mutilated because the more grotesque boys and girls receive more money from tourists—even though through their giving the tourists only encourage more mutilations.

- In 1995, 36.4 million Americans lived in poverty, according to the U.S. Bureau of Census, via the National Coalition for the Homeless. Forty percent of these were children.[8]

- The average American parent shops six hours a week but spends only forty minutes a week playing with the kids.[9]

- While the United States is one of the richest nations in the world, it ranks dead last (in percentage of GNP) among major Western donors of foreign aid.

- 1995 pizza sales in the United States soared to a record $31 billion—about five times the amount spent by the U.S. government on all international humanitarian and development assistance.[10]

- Worldwide, 1.3 billion people live on less than $1 a day (about the cost of a slice of New York City pizza).[11]

The depraved nature of humanity afflicts all of us. The Enron fallout merely displays on a very public stage our collective arrogance. The company's collapse reflects more than the failure of a few particular executives. Thousands of employees and millions of shareholders *wanted* the tale of Enron to be true because it fed their egos as well as their portfolios.

WHAT IS REQUIRED?

How the world has changed in just a few months! The very thing that not long ago prompted a surplus of arrogance now spurs agonizing regret.

In an interview with me, Tania Patel described her former pride as an Enron employee: "A year ago, I walked the streets of downtown arrogantly, believing everyone who knew I worked at Enron wished they were in my shoes. Why wouldn't this be the case—I worked in a high-tech building, was paid extremely well, ate at Houston's finest restaurants, and got to travel the country on Enron's tab on commercial airlines and the corporate jet."

That pride quickly turned to despair. "I felt like a part of me died on December 3, 2001," says Patel. "I was ripped away from the only corporate life I had known. Since then I have spent the majority of my time avoiding the Enron collapse issue. I rarely watch the news and the *Houston Chronicle* has become a source only of movie times and locations. Can anyone really blame me? Bombarded with questions like, 'Did you shred documents?' or 'Are you going to be in the August issue of *Playboy*?' has not been easy. The effects of my layoff all came to a head for me in late January. I was depressed—not just emotionally, but physically and spiritually as well."

Steve Lacey described to me the company's rapid transition,

fueled by its rapid rise in stock value. Employees who previously had no interest in the stock market became obsessed with their portfolios. His fellow employees suddenly tried to be day-traders because of their success with Enron.

"Oh! It was scary," recalls Lacey. "Here are people who are watching a stock go up and up and up; they were just frenzied. I mean, I'd walk in and there'd be at least one computer screen with the stock market on, live reports; guys sit there and watch it all day long like it was their favorite soap opera. It was always there: 'How'd the stock do today?' 'Oh, it's up to 89.' 'OK, good.' And this spurred some guys who thought they were going to make a killing in the market. There'd be these groups standing around, guys like me who climb power poles for a living, talking about becoming millionaires day-trading.

"I know some people who got hurt real bad. People used credit cards to keep buying stocks, you know, the fever was that bad. I know guys who went out and bought large amounts of Enron after it collapsed. One fellow lost $370,000 in his 401K, and he turned around and spent $45,000 of his own money to buy Enron at ten cents a share."

Greed drove not only a handful of Enron executives; it fueled the financial stampede of an entire country that began to believe the stock market could only continue to rise. Even Martha Stewart, the role model for etiquette and hospitality, now stands accused of illegally trading stocks with insider information.

When the court of the Creator comes to order, however, justice is assured. God has found us all guilty—and yet, despite a guilty verdict, God requires very little of us. And he has made his wishes clear:

> But he's already made it plain how to live, what to do,
> what GOD is looking for in men and women.

It's quite simple: Do what is fair and just to your neighbor,
　　be compassionate and loyal in your love,
And don't take yourself too seriously—
　　take God seriously.[12]

Will we learn from the mistakes of the Enron fallout and seek a simpler, more beautiful life? That's the ultimate question.

CHAPTER 16

The Antidote to Affluenza

In September of 1997 a remarkable one-hour television special called *Affluenza* first aired in the Pacific Northwest. Coproduced by Oregon Public Broadcasting and KCTS of Seattle, the program explored the high social and environmental costs of materialism and overconsumption. It defined *affluenza* as follows:

> **Af-flu-en-za** n. 1. The bloated, sluggish and unfulfilled feeling that results from efforts to keep up with the Joneses.
> 2. An epidemic of stress, overwork, waste and indebtedness caused by dogged pursuit of the American Dream. 3. An unsustainable addiction to economic growth.[1]

Some time later OPB and KCTS again joined forces to produce *Escape from Affluenza*, a solution-oriented sequel hosted by Wanda Urbanska, coauthor of *Simple Living*. Urbanska profiled people and organizations that choose to reduce consumption and waste by doing work that reflects their values and so helps them to live in better balance with the environment.

You may not have seen the program, but you may very well be asking the question posed by its producers: Is it possible for those living in an affluent culture to escape the disease of affluenza? I answer much the same as they did: Certainly! "Well then," you ask, "where can I find the antidote?"

For one, we find a cure in the wisdom of contemporary business executives who love people more than they do the bottom line. These men and women of faith challenge all of us to something better and higher.

But second, I would point us to a much older remedy. We can find a satisfying answer in the ancient monastic tradition of voluntary simplicity.

The simple values of monastics like St. Francis strongly confront the bankrupt values of our culture and offer us a life in which justice takes center stage. If we can exemplify justice in the world, then we can achieve a simplicity that will truly free us. The monastic fathers insist that true freedom lies in the abundance of life, *not* in the abundance of possessions. As a more modern monastic, Henry David Thoreau argued that going to the woods—whether literally or figuratively—allows us to confront what is truly essential in life. And almost always, we are going to discover that a simpler life brings us closer to nature, closer to authentic life, and closer to God.

A POLLUTED SEARCH FOR SPIRITUAL TRUTH

The modern chaos of garish neon signs calling us to all-you-can-eat pizza, nights of drug-induced semi-slumber, and the best products for the best prices cannot help but pollute our search for spiritual truth. In a quest for power and affluence, we have acquired things that now exercise power over us; we have become slaves to our belongings and they rule over us with brutal force. We must now work not just to earn our bread or support our families, but to pay off our houses, our cars, our boats and our big-screen TVs.

No wonder Jesus warned, "Take care! Protect yourself against the least bit of greed. Life is not defined by what you have, even when you have a lot."[2]

The hard-learned lessons of Enron can benefit the living room as well as the boardroom. Who can deny that "regular people" have fallen prey to the same lust for power, possessions, and status—along with a blatant disregard for the surrounding community—that poisoned Enron? Who can argue that in American society, even among Christians (perhaps *especially* among Christians), we have come to define success solely on the basis of how much money we make and how many bedrooms we have in our houses?

On our journey to become whole and healthy people, we must inevitably travel a path that leads toward simplicity. We begin to find contentment when we devote ourselves to acquiring only what we need. And what do we do with the rest? We give it away for the benefit of others, as yet another wise man suggested:

> Our desire is not that others might be relieved while you are hard pressed, but that there might be equality. At the present time your plenty will supply what they need, so that in turn their plenty will supply what you need. Then there will be equality, as it is written: "He who gathered much did not have too much, and he who gathered little did not have too little."[3]

Of course, to freely give away what we do not need seems radical to the ears of Western culture. We've come to believe that wealth is not simply a gift from God, but a sign of God's favor. To give a little something to charity every once in awhile, great; Enron CEO Ken Lay papered Houston with charity donations. But to freely give away a substantial wad of cash when you could buy a complete home-theater system with it? Why? And anyway, how can you tell when you have too much? Just who determines what you "need"?

I admit that the line between excessive wealth and simplicity may be hard to find. Certainly we can argue that Ken Lay had too much money, as did his cohorts, Skilling and Fastow. But is it possible that we too have too much?

You can begin to find that line by asking a few simple questions. Do I *need* another car? If so, does it have to be a *new* car? How much house is too much? How many pairs of shoes are too many?

No one else can make these decisions for you. Only you can make them, based on your personal convictions and conscience. The challenge is to move into the tension of balancing your desires with the reality of your community and the rest of the world. This means that shopping, as simple entertainment, should become increasingly less appealing. And it also means that researching purchases should become more complicated than simply seeking the greatest value or the highest visibility. What about the moral consequences? Community consequences? Environmental consequences?

Want an example where the environmental consequences outweigh intrinsic value? Then consider Hardi-Plank siding, the current rage in new-home construction. Hardi-Plank is almost indestructible and relatively inexpensive—but its manufacture harms the environment and those who install it breathe in dangerous toxic fumes.[4] We ought to weigh such factors as we consider one product over another. In this example, brick might become the best choice; despite a slightly higher price, it is made quite simply (and safely) from earth, water, and fire. Or you might consider recycling old building materials or using new "green" building techniques to design a home made from adobe, straw-bale, rammed-earth, or other earth-friendly alternatives.

Almost every buying decision will take on an added dimension when you practice conscious consumerism. When you buy at a large retail chain, a chain electronics store, or a restaurant with locations all across the country, you may be getting the lowest price on a familiar product. But you may also be contributing to the decline of unique community businesses or encouraging the further exploitation of laborers in Mexico or China. The business from whom you buy may have a division that makes weapons of mass destruction, a record of global environmental opportunism, or dealings with a repressive regime in a distant land. When you realize that in your purchases you make choices that impact yourself, your community, and individuals you may never even meet, your responsibility to shop intelligently becomes crystal clear.

THE BIRTHPLACE OF SIMPLICITY

"Living simply" means that we carefully examine what it means to fully live. How? By focusing our efforts on things true, beautiful, and essential—things like family, faith, health, creation.

In my family, simplicity means that we eat natural and organic foods, purchase used and recycled goods and clothes, and have our children play with only wooden and "natural" toys. I pray that my family's current convictions will expand and mature as I learn and grow.

Contentment is the birthplace of a simple life. When you feel content with what you have, you don't feel the need to strive for increasing numbers of things. The writer to the Hebrews gave his readers some helpful advice along these lines:

Keep your lives free from the love of money and be content
with what you have, because God has said,
"Never will I leave you; never will I forsake you."[5]

Treasures lose much of their power over you when you see God as
your greatest treasure. Following that line of thought, a much earlier
writer, King David, articulated his own journey toward simplicity:

God, I'm not trying to rule the roost,
I don't want to be king of the mountain.
I haven't meddled where I have no business
    or fantasized grandiose plans.
I've kept my feet on the ground,
I've cultivated a quiet heart.
Like a baby content in its mother's arms,
    my soul is a baby content.[6]

Contrary to what many think, the simple life is born in the
green fields of contentment, not the brown pastures of asceticism.
The Bible never separates the physical from the spiritual. Many
Christians embrace the gnostic heresy that material things are evil.
Not so! Remember, it was *God* who provided man with every luxury in the Garden of Eden. God gave the beauty of creation to
Adam and later called his chosen people to a Promised Land flowing with milk and honey. Real simplicity does not come from
begrudgingly denying yourself the delights of creation, but from
finding contentment in the gifts God lavishes upon you, helping to
make them available to all people. This sets you free to take full
pleasure in life.

THE SIMPLE LIFE AT ITS MOST SATISFYING

The most satisfying kind of true simplicity may be found in a life of deep faith and devotion, beginning with the contemplative disciplines of prayer and meditation. Through these disciplines God can move us beyond our own fluctuating desires to find true happiness. One author wrote of the deep satisfaction to be found in a life of faith and devotion and then declared:

> The deepest, most satisfying delights God gives us through creation are free gifts from nature and from loving relationships with people. After your basic needs are met, accumulated money begins to diminish your capacity for these pleasures rather than increase them. Buying things contributes absolutely nothing to the heart's capacity for joy.
>
> There is a deep difference between the temporary thrill of a new toy and a homecoming hug from a devoted friend. Who do you think has the deepest, most satisfying joy in life, the man who pays $340 for a fortieth-floor suite downtown and spends his evening in the half-lit, smoke-filled lounge impressing strange women with ten-dollar cocktails, or the man who chooses the Motel 6 by a vacant lot of sunflowers and spends his evening watching the sunset and writing a love letter to his wife?[7]

Do you want to be happy? Then don't spend your life in the frantic acquisition of things. "No one can serve two masters," Jesus said. "For you will hate one and love the other, or be devoted to the one and despise the other. You cannot serve both God and money. . . . So don't worry about having enough food or drink or clothing. Why be like the pagans who are so deeply concerned about these things? Your heavenly Father already knows all your needs."[8]

Paul warned his young protégé Timothy in a similar way. "People who long to be rich fall into temptation and are trapped by many foolish and harmful desires that plunge them into ruin and destruction," the apostle said. "For the love of money is at the root of all kinds of evil. And some people, craving money, have wandered from the faith and pierced themselves with many sorrows."[9] The wrongheaded belief that wealth solves all problems drives us to create riches that inevitably bring a new and more challenging set of problems. Why go through that kind of agony when you can enjoy the simple life at its most satisfying through a growing devotion to the God of the universe?

Sometimes we get sucked into a barren and consumptive lifestyle by listening too attentively to the marketing messages we see on TV, hear on the radio, and read in magazines and newspapers. We forget too easily that advertising campaigns portray their products as much more than they really are. Madison Avenue presents clothes, food, and household cleaning supplies as sources of joy with the potential to heal and fulfill us, to fill the void in our hearts. Author Mark Buchanan describes this pervasive lie in his winning essay on consumerism:

> One of the strangest ads I ever saw was a television commercial for Kool-Aid. It showed a bunch of kids sitting slumped and sullen on a gorgeous summer day. They're bored, numbed with it. It's almost a portrait of suicidal despair. Why go on living? Then the mother brings out a round, dew-beaded pitcher of Kool-Aid, ruby red and jiggling with ice. The kids go crazy. They leap, they clap, they cheer, they run, they gulp. This, yes this, is something to live for! The impression we're given is that the exuberance over that moment lives long past

the moment: that there is something redemptive about the pitcher of Kool-Aid, that it restores purpose and hope to all of life. Well, my own children like Kool-Aid. Just not that much.[10]

Kool-Aid, of course, cannot bring lasting happiness to anyone; that much seems obvious. So then, by what cranial contortion do we convince ourselves that where Kool-Aid fails, boats and cars and houses and clothes and jewelry and entertainment systems and a thousand other items may succeed? They may cost more than Kool-Aid, but they possess not one more erg of power to bring us the contentment we seek. God reserves that kind of happiness for a devoted relationship with himself.

USING WEALTH TO PURSUE JUSTICE

When one comes to see money and wealth as a means to an end rather than the end itself, then one can tap newly freed-up wealth to pursue justice.

Shane Claiborne, with the Simple Way community in Philadelphia, has made this life-altering shift. During a protest on behalf of the homeless in his city, a police officer assaulted Shane; some time later Shane received a thirty-thousand-dollar settlement from the city. So what did he do with this money? He immediately began to dream of how he might give it away.

Shane sent the first ten grand to ministries across the world that work with the poor. He then brought the remaining cash to Wall Street, where he and his friends gave it all away to the needy on New York's streets.

Why did Shane do what he did? He gave away every dime of his thirty thousand dollars out of a deep, biblical desire to do justice.

Could he have used those funds in a more productive way? Perhaps; but it was his call to make, and he made it the best way he knew how. The real question is not, "Could Shane have more effectively used that money?" but, "How am I using the funds God has entrusted to me to do justice in my sphere of influence?"

Peter Gomes, the pastor for Harvard University, reminds us that to whom much is given, much is expected, and that "giving in this sense of expectation is not optional, it is the requirement of wealth."[11] Because God has made us an object of charity, Gomes argues, we are obliged to care for those around us who are in need.

Every one of us can be a source of justice or oppression. Let us pray that God will show us how to "let justice roll down like waters, and righteousness like an ever flowing stream."[12] A famous monk born more than eight centuries ago dedicated most of his adult life to seeing justice roll down like waters—and he can inspire us to keep on doing justice yet today.

THE MODEL OF ST. FRANCIS

The journey of St. Francis from financial affluence to a life spent investing in spiritual prosperity continues to inspire awe. His work challenges all people of faith to give their lives away in service to others.

Francis, son of a wealthy Italian cloth merchant named Pietro de Bernardone, was born at Assisi in A.D. 1181. At his birth his mother gave him the name John, but his father changed the boy's name to Francis upon returning from a business trip.

The family trade provided Francis with all the physical things he needed and he spent freely, overindulging himself and his friends. In 1202, however, at the age of twenty-one, Francis spent a year in

Perugia as a prisoner of war. Not long after his release he contracted a serious illness, during which he began to reflect on the barren state of his soul and the vanity of his riches. Still, at that time he only began the process; his conversion took much longer. Francis spent the next three years spending lavishly, entertaining himself and his friends and denying himself no pleasure.

At age twenty-four, Francis joined the armies of Walter of Brienne to fight for the pope. One night while camped at Spoleto, Francis had a vision of the Lord. A voice asked him, "Who can benefit you the most, the Lord or the servant? Why do you desert the Lord for his vassal?" The vision overwhelmed Francis, and he abandoned the army to return home. This late-night visitation prompted Francis to contemplate his soul and challenged him to live in greater simplicity.

In time, Francis felt altogether unconcerned with wealth; increasingly he concerned himself only with the poor and needy. He exchanged his clothes with a vagabond and began begging in the streets of Assisi, only to give to the poor everything he had received. Francis even took fabric from his father's shop, selling it all at the town market. He also sold the horse he'd been riding and gave the proceeds to the poor, a hospitable yet undignified act that infuriated his father. Pietro angrily took his son to the bishop of Assisi and demanded that the cleric order Francis to return the money. The bishop warned Francis not to steal, not even from his own family. No sooner had the bishop's order left his mouth than Francis stripped himself naked and placed all his belongings before his father.

"Up to now," Francis declared, "I have called Pietro di Bernardone father. Hereafter I shall not say, 'Father Pietro di Bernardone,' but 'Our Father Who Art in Heaven!'"

The bishop felt so moved by Francis's confession that he placed his own cloak over the young man. But Francis quickly fled the cathedral to meet his fellow beggars in the street. In this way he decisively broke from his father and all that he associated with his father: wealth, comfort, and power. From then on he chose a life of simplicity.

Francis did not plan to create a religious order, but over time, many like-minded men began to follow him. Soon it became clear that their common mission required organization. The more the group grew, the more Francis had to delegate responsibility to others. After writing a detailed "rule of order" for his group, Francis left for the mountains to live in secluded prayer. There, after extended fasting, he reportedly received the stigmata, the wounds of Christ. He returned to visit the Franciscans and later died at the Porziuncula on October 3, 1226.

Francis embodied a life of simplicity, poverty, and humility before God and man. He saw the poor and needy as a part of his own family. Francis inspired thousands of individuals during his lifetime, and his story of authentic faith lives on in his writings and prayers. May we learn from Francis and join him in a prayer he offered, to help us get beyond our own selfishness and greed:

> O Divine Master, grant that I may not so much seek
>> to be consoled
>>> as to console;
>> To be understood
>>> as to understand;
>> To be loved
>>> as to love.
>>> For it is in giving that we receive;
>>> It is in pardoning that we are pardoned;
>>> And it is in dying that we are born to eternal life.

In Search of an Honorable and Satisfying Life

The Tao of Enron ultimately is about the choices we make, not the infamous business failures that marked the end of the twentieth century and the beginning of the twenty-first. Every day each one of us has the opportunity to choose a path that leads to abundance and beauty.

Many in our culture possess the mind and abilities needed to make money—sometimes large sums of money. And for this no one needs to feel ashamed. Such gifts come as a blessing from the Creator, who grants some the brains for business, or the singing voice of an angel, or the vision of an entrepreneur, or the steady hand of a championship golfer, or the eye of a sculptor. "Every good and perfect gift is from above," say the Scriptures, "coming down from the Father of the heavenly lights, who does not change like shifting shadows."[1]

The Bible clearly teaches that "If you're a hard worker and do a good job, you deserve your pay; we don't call your wages a gift."[2] Fair compensation is both biblical and right. If Gordon Bethune can turn Continental Airlines—once considered the worst airline in the industry—into the most profitable hub and spoke carrier in the land, a company that continually ranks at the top of its field in customer service, then he and his coworkers deserve to be well-compensated.

The issue is not wealth; it is the way we use that wealth and our motives for acquiring it. We have to begin asking ourselves a crucial question: What kind of future will our actions bequeath to the men and women who will follow us?

THE TIME HAS COME

The time has come to pause and consider the inheritance you will leave for future generations—not your financial bequest, but the legacy of a journey worth furthering.

We all stand at a precipice. Most of us remain blind to our own sin—and how close we stand to the "dark side"! It was Ken Lay, interviewed just months before Enron's failure made the headlines, who described integrity in no uncertain terms:

> When I talk about integrity as one of our values, I usually talk about absolute integrity, as though it needs to be qualified. It is really always doing the right thing. Not bending the rules, not cutting the corners, not doing things that are illegal or immoral. I think that fits my faith, but it's also good business. But indeed, I don't find it difficult. And we have been in countries where it became apparent that you couldn't do business without bribing somebody and we just pulled out. We will leave a country before we will compromise our values.[3]

It sounds great, doesn't it? But as we have seen, integrity is far easier to talk about than to exhibit. Not only did Ken Lay ignore the warnings of Sherron Watkins' pointed memo, but he also pondered the ramifications of firing her after she came forward to blow the whistle.[4]

THE PAYOFF FOR HUMILITY

Probably you will never have the "opportunity" to make millions on your company's stock through insider information. But rest assured, if you are padding the expense account, twisting the truth for your own purposes, or adopting a "me-first" mentality, you *will* capitulate when the opportune time arrives. Listen to the ironic advice Ken Lay offered to young businesspeople as he stood at the brink of his company's collapse:

> There is no conflict between having a very strong religious faith and being a very successful person in business. I think the main thing that anybody that has a strong faith should do is practice it, live it, share it, and, obviously, do a good job at whatever they are doing. Don't feel that it's something they need to conceal, or hide, or not practice if they're going to be successful. They will probably be put in circumstances from time to time that aren't exactly what they would like to see, but they should not be bashful about leaving those circumstances, changing that particular job or whatever else.[5]

You can bet that Ken Lay now regrets he didn't walk away earlier—and he and many others had good reason to walk. Accountants reportedly shredded the books they were hired to keep; stock analysts employed to defend investors fell asleep at the wheel; and lawyers allegedly destroyed the truth they swore to defend.

Before investigators got hot on Enron's trail, an ocean of digital information detailing its corporate misbehavior evaporated in an electronic drought. During the summer of 2002, an overworked Information Technology (IT) department changed Enron's e-mail software from Outlook to Lotus. The downside of this planned changeover? All e-mails left unprotected would be destroyed.

At least one IT manager questioned the wisdom of such a software replacement; he thought Outlook worked just fine. He pressed the issue with his superiors, only to discover the changeover had nothing to do with the merits of the respective accounting packages. The switch took place on direct orders from Enron's legal department. And so many executives celebrated the disappearance of years of vital and potentially damning electronic information, believing the modern mantra that "you're not guilty if you don't get caught."

WHAT TO DO NOW?

In the light of the Enron scandal, we all ought to be asking ourselves a crucial question. How can *I* avoid the lure of greed and power?

In attempting to answer my own question, I have to admit that I know of no easy answers. So far as I know, no simple, three-step solution exists. Yet because we must begin somewhere, I suggest we start with a recommitment to our consciences. Let each of us purposefully tune into our conscience and heed our internal moral compass. If we turn away from the inner voice that calls us back to the right path, before we know it we will find ourselves in a pitch-black forest with no sign of a safe road leading back into the light. Therefore, you and I must do whatever may be necessary to nurture that inner voice. Let us stop routinely to examine our lives and the important decisions we make.

Second, we have no choice but to abandon the incessant lust for more and instead develop a life of contentment. The book of Hebrews reminds us,

> Don't be obsessed with getting more material things. Be relaxed with what you have. Since God assured us, 'I'll never let you down, never walk off and leave you,' we can boldly quote, 'God is there, ready to help; I'm fearless no matter what. Who or what can get to me?'"[6]

Contentment breaks the power of envy and avarice and opens the door to genuine thankfulness and joy.

Last, we must never forget our own propensity for evil. None of us are innately any better than the so-called traitors of Enron. Why should we vilify Ken Lay or Jeff Skilling, when any of us could be either of them? We all flirt with ethical dangers and at times cross the line that leads into a moral abyss. We avoid our own destruction only through a lifelong struggle won in the trenches of humility.

May we all abandon the vanities of chasing after wealth and selfish gain and instead follow the timeless wisdom of Proverbs:

> The payoff for humility and a respect for the things of God is honor and a satisfying life.[7]

McFaith: The Gospel at 50 Percent Off

Enron turned everything into a commodity. What most of us once considered trash — even something like recycled newsprint — Enron turned into a treasure to be bought low and sold high.

And the church has learned. Listen to the sobering indictment of David Wells:

> We have turned to a God that we can use rather than to a God we must obey; we have turned to a God who will fulfill our needs rather than to a God before whom we must surrender our rights to ourselves. He is a God for us, for our satisfaction — not because we have learned to think of him in this way through Christ, but because we have learned to think of him this way through the marketplace. In the marketplace, everything is for us, for our pleasure, for our satisfaction, and we have come to assume that it must be so in the church as well. And so we transform the God of mercy into a God who is at our mercy.[1]

COMMODIFYING THE GOSPEL

Sadly, many communities of faith have followed Enron's lead and have commodified the gospel. They have transformed the good news into a marketable and saleable good, in the process largely abandoning the historic and biblical truth that "it is the power of God for the salvation of everyone who believes."[2] Instead they offer a product to fit individual tastes and felt needs.

The music minister of one of Houston's largest evangelical churches, for example, believes that no church can do without marketing, including his: "People think because we're a church, maybe we shouldn't market," he says. "But any organization, secular or otherwise, if [it's] going to grow, [it's] got to get people to buy into the product."[3]

The American church appears to be rapidly adopting the hollow values of a capitalism run amok. Religion has become Big Business — and faith in Christ has been made into a product to market and sell (after conducting strategic demographic and socioeconomic surveys, of course). Tragically, those who buy never receive instruction or even encouragement on how to count the cost of their purchase.[4]

The late, former chaplain of the U.S. Senate, Richard Halverson, offered a valuable historical perspective:

> In the beginning the church was a fellowship of men
> and women centering on the living Christ. Then the
> church moved to Greece where it became a philosophy.
> Then it moved to Rome where it became an institution.
> Next, it moved to Europe where it became a culture.
> And, finally, it moved to America where it became an
> enterprise.[5]

And so Jesus has become a product, his people a sales team. Pastors have shed their biblical roles as shepherds to become CEOs of religious corporations. The same Christ who violently threw profiteers out of the temple has somehow become wed to a church that thrives on marketing schemes, televangelist propaganda, and a cottage industry of religious paraphernalia (such as Jesus shoelaces, Jesus t-shirts, Jesus pencils, and testa-mints). Church buildings no longer strive for the transcendence of grand cathedrals; instead they long to emulate shopping malls offering consumers a plethora of choices in worship styles, easily accessible parking, self-help theology, clean bathrooms, and cleverly marketed products for every age group. It appears that Jesus has a new image consultant charged with making him appealing at any cost.

And it breaks the Father's heart.

God will have none of this. "Only God Himself makes the Gospel attractive in a person," says one commentator, "and He does so through the power and working of the Holy Spirit. The Holy Spirit will not be bought, sold, bartered, or traded. He comes on His own terms whenever and wherever He wills" (John 2:8).[6] Years ago Karl Barth spoke prophetically to current market-driven adaptations of Christianity:

> The word of God is not for sale; and therefore it has no need
> of shrewd salesmen. The word of God is not seeking patrons;
> therefore it refuses price-cutting and bargaining; therefore it
> has no need of middlemen. The word of God does not com-
> pete with other commodities that are being offered to men
> on the bargain counter of life. It does not care to be sold at
> any price. It desires only to be its own genuine self, without
> being compelled to suffer alterations and modifications. . . .

It will, however, not stop to overcome resistance with bargain counter methods. Promoters' success are sham victories; their crowded churches and the breathlessness of their audiences have nothing in common with the word of God.[7]

The man in charge of parking at another Houston megachurch largely ignores Barth's counsel. He explains his church's philosophy this way: "You know the saying: 'The customer's always right.' We've kind of employed that theme, which I think is excellent, much like a fine hotel or country club."[8]

THE CHALLENGE AHEAD

The challenge for people of faith lies in reconciling the teachings of Scripture with the demands of a consumer culture. While a world filled with competing products tries to re-envision God through its own lenses, a decision to become a "Christian Consumer" stands in total contradiction to the Great Commandment to love God and one's neighbor as oneself.

And in any event we have to ask ourselves a question: Who would buy a product that demands we forsake, not coddle, our own selfish desires?

SECTION ONE: GETTING FAMILIAR WITH THE ISSUES
(INTRODUCTION, CHAPTERS ONE AND TWO)

1. How much do you know about the Enron case? Describe what you have heard.

2. What is your general impression of what happened at Enron? What do you think went wrong?

3. Have you or anyone you know been hurt personally by the Enron collapse? If so, briefly describe the situation.

4. How well do you understand the American system of capitalism? Describe your current understanding. Is it based on greed, as some say? Explain.

5. Do you think capitalism improves the American quality of life, or do you think it creates a wedge between the classes? Explain.

6. Is it possible to keep greed from corrupting American capitalism? If so, how do you think this could be done?

7. Name some symptoms of greed that you see in your workplace. How has it affected your company? How has it affected *you*? What steps can you take to escape its lure?

8. What values ought to guide and direct the business activities of followers of Christ? How are these values supposed to *practically* shape how Christians live and work in the marketplace?

SECTION TWO: CONNECTING FAITH TO LIFE
(CHAPTERS THREE AND FOUR)

1. How does your own faith affect the way you conduct yourself in the workplace?
2. In what way(s) does the faith of Ken Lay (as described in the book) resemble your own? Explain.
3. Do you consider any areas of your life more "spiritual" than others? Explain.
4. How would you describe the idea of "dualism" to someone else?
5. Explain the idea of "isolated beliefs." Do you hold any "isolated beliefs"? Explain.
6. In what ways do you see dualism expressed in the general culture? In your workplace? In your church? In your own life?
7. What do you think is the antidote for dualism?
8. In a Bible, read Proverbs 16:3, 1 Corinthians 10:31, and Colossians 3:17. What do these verses have to say about dualism? How do they recommend that believers respond to dualism?

SECTION THREE: CHOOSING HUMILITY OVER PRIDE
(CHAPTERS FIVE AND SIX)

1. Would you consider yourself a proud person? Explain. Would others agree with your self-assessment? Explain.
2. Would you consider Jeff Skilling a proud person? In your opinion, how did his pride (or lack of it) affect his job performance?
3. Name some examples of destructive pride that you have seen in the workplace.

4. Some theologians believe that pride is the worst of all sins. Do you agree? Explain.

5. How has pride affected your finances? Relationships? Family? Faith?

6. How would you define humility?

7. Describe the most humble person you know. Do you like this person? Explain.

8. The Bible claims that God hates human pride (Leviticus 26:19, 2 Chronicles 26:16, James 4:6). Why should this be so? What is it about human arrogance that invites God's judgment?

SECTION FOUR: DOES POWER CORRUPT?
(CHAPTERS SEVEN AND EIGHT)

1. In what areas of your life do you exert significant power? How do you generally use that power?

2. Do you think that a desire for power drove Rebecca Mark? Explain.

3. Discuss the adage "Power corrupts, and absolute power corrupts absolutely." Do you agree with this idea? Why or why not?

4. Describe someone you know whom you believe has lusted for power. How did others react to this person? How did you react?

5. Are there any areas of your life in which you lust for power? Explain. What would you do with this power if you got it?

6. Name at least five consequences of the lust for power in the lives of those most directly affected by the one seeking such power. Try to avoid the abstract and be as concrete as possible.

7. In your experience, what usually has happened to a person who lusts for power? Be as specific as you can.

8. Read Jesus' words in Matthew 20:25-28. How do his statements there relate to the lust for power? How does he suggest that his followers confront this lust in their own lives? What does this suggest for you, personally?

SECTION FIVE: IMMEDIATE GRATIFICATION
VS. LONG-TERM THINKING
(CHAPTERS NINE AND TEN)

1. Do you ever struggle with issues of immediate gratification? Explain.

2. How does it appear that a desire for immediate gratification got Andrew Fastow in trouble?

3. Name several pressures in our culture to "get it *now*."

4. In what area(s) of your life are you most impatient? Explain.

5. How has your impatience negatively affected your life? Give at least one example.

6. How can you combat the urge to "get it *now*"? What strategies have you, your friends, or acquaintances used?

7. How often do you engage in "long-term thinking"? What areas of your life might most benefit from such thinking? What keeps you from such long-term thinking?

8. In a Bible read Proverbs 13:22, 21:5, and 31:20-25. What do these texts say about the benefits of long-term thinking? Why can the woman described in the last passage "laugh at the days to come"? What changes, if any, do these passages suggest you ought to make?

SECTION SIX: LOOKING OUT FOR NUMBER ONE?
(CHAPTERS ELEVEN AND TWELVE)

1. Why is it often hard for a single individual to "blow the whistle" on wrongdoing?
2. Why do you think Sherron Watkins blew the whistle on Enron? What motivated her?
3. If we are more concerned about the welfare of groups of people than we are about our own advantage, does it get easier to blow the whistle when necessary? Explain.
4. What does the author mean by "individualism"?
5. In what ways is individualism good? How is it bad?
6. What do you believe God thinks of individualism? Explain.
7. Does individualism belong in the church? Explain.
8. In the Bible read Galatians 5:14-15, Philippians 2:3-4, and 1 John 3:17-18. What do these passages teach us about individualism? What do they suggest as a remedy? How can you seek to put these texts into practice in your own life, especially in your business?

SECTION SEVEN: CHOOSING ONE'S ROAD
(CHAPTERS THIRTEEN AND FOURTEEN)

1. Have business pressures ever driven you to consider suicide? If so, explain.
2. Does the story of J. Clifford Baxter cause you to ponder how fleeting life is? Explain.
3. In the Bible read James 4:13-17. What does this passage say about the fleeting nature of life? How does it suggest we deal with it? Do you think this is good or bad advice? Explain.

4. Do you feel fulfilled in your own work? Explain.

5. What two factors motivated Chris Bryan to first consider, and then change, his business career? Have these two factors ever influenced you? Explain.

6. Chris Bryan left a good-paying job to enroll in a theological school. Do you think he made a good decision? Why or why not? Why do you think he had some doubts about his decision?

7. Is a career in ministry morally better than a career in business? Explain. What would an affirmative answer to the question mean for the author's earlier discussion in chapter four about dualism?

SECTION EIGHT: WHERE ARE WE HEADED?
(Chapters Fifteen and Sixteen)

1. What do you think God would say to you if *you* were on trial?

2. If you knew you had to stand before God in heaven's courtroom, would that knowledge change the way you live now? Explain.

3. What does a life of "simplicity" mean to you? Is it required for Christians? Explain.

4. How could you simplify your life? Name several specific things you could do in the next couple of days.

5. How could the church simplify its life? What would a more simple church look like? Do you think this new church would be more attractive to unchurched people, or more unattractive? Explain.

6. What things do you really need? Do you think you have enough? Explain.

7. What does "generosity" mean to you? Do you consider yourself a generous person? Explain.

8. Read in the Bible Psalm 112:5, Proverbs 11:25, and 1 Timothy 6:17-19. What, if anything, do these passages say about a simple life? What do they teach about generosity? Do they challenge you in any way? Explain.

SECTION NINE: BONUS ROUND

1. What would you do if you were caught or implicated in unethical activities?

2. What would you do if you found out your married boss was having an affair with a coworker?

3. What would you do if you had information that could cause your employer serious legal trouble?

4. What would you do if your entire savings and retirement funds had been tied to Enron stock when it fell?

5. Imagine that following several short-term developmental assignments, you are offered a position as a corporate officer. You know you do not have many of the qualifications of an ideal candidate, but you seem highly regarded and are offered a combination of compensation and perks beyond your wildest dreams. What do you do?

6. Would more legislation make corporate executives more ethical? Explain.

7. Describe how you felt when you thought someone you trusted did something illegal or immoral.

8. What lessons from the Enron case have most impacted you? Describe any changes they may have caused you to make or consider making.

9. What does good resource management look like to you? In business? In the home? In the church?

10. Read in the Bible Psalm 50:7-23. How does it change our perspective when we realize God owns literally *everything*? How does God want this knowledge to change the way we operate?

A Few Suggestions for Simple Living

As you contemplate what simplicity may mean for you, consider a few suggested guidelines that may get you thinking in a helpful direction:

- Think before you buy; analyze your motives for making a purchase.
- Refuse to become a slave to another's expectations. If you sense that someone else's opinions are pressuring you to make a purchase, hold off on your decision to buy. Acquire what you need, not what your neighbors think you need.
- Reject a mindless response to advertising and begin to exercise power over your buying and spending habits. In this way you open the door to real freedom.
- Avoid the latest technology; it usually costs too much and rarely ends up being worth anything close to what you paid.
- Avoid anything addictive. The apostle Paul declares, "I will not be mastered by anything."[1] Did you know that the global economy makes its real money from addiction? Consider three of the strongest forces in the American economy: tobacco, caffeine

drinks (Coca-Cola and Pepsi make up a large percentage of the GDP), and illegal drugs. I have spent untold amounts of money on soda as the distribution mechanism of my drug of choice: caffeine. In 1999, I finally broke my own addictive cycle (and watched Dr. Pepper stock plummet!).

- Seek opportunities to give and receive nothing in return. Instead of involving yourself or your family in another social activity, consider volunteering in the community. Kids need to grow up with a model of charity. You can help keep a woman's shelter or a food bank going by volunteering, in addition to any financial contribution you might make. You can help with the books, write a grant, answer a phone, paint a wall, or help customers in a thrift store. All those tasks are important. Chances are they'll find things that the kids can do, too.

- Avoid items like cheaply manufactured clothes or other consumer goods that capitalize on groups of oppressed people. According to a World Bank study released in 1996, 1.3 billion people live on less than one dollar a day and three billion people live on less than two dollars a day. Decisions that we make regarding our lifestyle and finances have global implications. Don't support injustice. Anywhere.

- Purchase products that directly benefit the poor and oppressed around the world. Support direct interventions into their lives instead of those suggested by agencies and corporations. Most of the billions loaned to Third World nations by the IMF and the World Bank have enriched greedy politicians and American corporations, not the intended recipients, who nonetheless get shackled to a lifetime of onerous debt repayments.

- Live in community, where you can learn to help and serve your neighbors. Groups that devote their resources to the members of the group spare themselves great expense. It's possible to own cars, lawnmowers, DVDs, tools, bikes, and even homes in community. In this way you will experience the benefits of a shared life.

- Reduce your consumption of nonrenewable natural resources by sharing books, appliances, tools, sports equipment, and so on. Patronize your library instead of buying books; make friends with a local video rental store instead of buying videos. Learn that you can *use* things without having to *own* them.

- Adopt giving as a lifestyle; it may breathe renewed hope into a world filled with the extremely rich and the extremely poor. Dr. Charles Birch once said, "The rich must live more simply that the poor may simply live."

- Reduce your food budget by gardening, joining a food co-op, and fasting regularly. Americans overeat compulsively; if you can't forget what your mother said about clearing your plate, then at least put less food on it.

- Set, and keep, a monthly budget. Overspending is often a result of underplanning.

- Lower your family's energy consumption by walking or utilizing public transportation, bicycles, or car pools. By trading away a little convenience, you will help the planet. And accustom your children to using these alternate forms of transportation so that they will seem natural as they grow older.

- Depending on the climate where you live, consider buying a fan instead of an air conditioner. Open your windows. Capture a breeze.

- Plant a tree. Or two. Or three. Especially if you live in a city or suburb. Trees help reduce pollution, lower ambient temperatures, and beautify the world for all of us, rich and poor alike.

- Consider alternate, renewable sources of energy. Many people can now get solar power, and hybrid gas/electric cars should soon be within reach of many consumers. An investment in clean power will pay off in years of less pollution and less consumption. And encourage these energy ideas in your community and beyond; corporations have a vested interest in keeping us shackled to petroleum and coal and gas-guzzling vehicles, and their campaign contributions and lobbyists speak loudly. We must speak louder.
- Recycle, reuse, and renew. Buy recyclable batteries, reuse plastic and paper sacks, use curbside recycling. There are countless tiny ways you can reduce consumption and help the planet.
- Spend real time with your family. Read, talk, cook dinner together. Don't substitute busyness (going to a movie, a mall, out to dinner) for real contact. Play with your kids. Rake the lawn together. Remember that your work, your status in the community—in fact, everything the world counts important—pales in significance next to the people God has placed in your life. No one will remember ten years from now that you stayed late to finish off an account. But someone may remember that you came home early to play touch football.
- Enjoy what is free: town concerts, lectures at local universities, parks, and nature preserves. The list is endless if you pay attention.
- Live creatively.

The voluntary simplicity movement has mushroomed in the past few years, creating a wealth of resources designed to help interested individuals to simplify their lives. The development of the Internet has made possible much of this growth. Consider just three sites that provide a vast number of ideas and perspectives on simple living:

- www.simpleliving.org. The organization behind this faith-based site began in 1973 as a protest against the increasing commercialization of Christmas.
- www.simpleliving.net. This group has created a comprehensive tool for interested readers called "The Web of Simplicity."
- www.gallagherpress.com/pierce/reading.htm. This web page brings up a 92-book bibliography on simple living compiled by Linda Breen Pierce.

If you're truly interested in a simpler lifestyle, the best advice I can give is this: Try something new. Don't merely think about a simple life; take steps now—small ones at first, if necessary—to declutter your life and discover the joy of living based on what you need. And now let me leave you with an old Jewish proverb that might get you thinking:

Where there is too much . . . something is missing.

INTRODUCTION

1. See Matthew 7:13-14.
2. Revelation 18:19, MSG.
3. Ecclesiastes 5:10-17, MSG.
4. James 5:3, MSG.

CHAPTER 1

1. http://www.salon.com/tech/feature/2002/01/23/enron_toll/index1.html
2. http://www.salon.com/tech/feature/2002/01/23/enron_toll/index1.html
3. http://www.salon.com/tech/feature/2002/01/23/enron_toll/index1.html
4. http://www.salon.com/tech/feature/2002/01/23/enron_toll/index1.html
5. http://www.senate.gov/~commerce/hearings/121801Farmer.pdf
6. http://www.ourfuture.org/articles/20020603081816.pdf
7. http://www.salon.com/tech/feature/2002/01/23/enron_toll/
8. http://www.senate.gov/~commerce/hearings/121801Farmer.pdf
9. http://www.senate.gov/~commerce/hearings/121801Farmer.pdf
10. http://www.guardian.co.uk/enron/story/0,11337,637351,00.html
11. Brian Cruver, *Anatomy of Greed* (New York: Carroll & Graf, 2002), p. 1.
12. James 1:11, MSG.
13. See Genesis 1:28.
14. Revelation 11:18.

CHAPTER TWO

1. David Barboza, "Friends Say Ex-Chief Despairs, Seeking Someone to Believe Him," *New York Times*, August 22, 2002.
2. Mark Gimein, "The Greedy Bunch," *Fortune*, September 2, 2002. Found at www.fortune.com/insiders/companies.html
3. http://www.guardian.co.uk/g2/story/0,3604,825351,00.html

4. http://www.rockymountainnews.com/drmn/state/article/
0,1299,DRMN_21_989268,00.html

5. James 5:1-6, MSG.

6. Luke 12:15.

7. Ecclesiastes 2:10-11.

8. Romans 8:32.

9. Deuteronomy 8:11-18, MSG.

10. See Numbers 11:18-20.

11. Ralph Winter, "Reconsecration to a Wartime, not a Peacetime, Lifestyle," *Perspectives on the World Christian Movement* (Pasadena: William Carey Library, 1981), p. 814.

12. Dr. Martin Luther King Jr., "Nobel Prize Acceptance Speech," *I Have a Dream* (New York: HarperCollins, 1992), p. 110.

13. Ecclesiastes 5:10.

14. 1 Timothy 6:10.

15. 1 Timothy 6:9-10, MSG.

16. John Piper, *Desiring God:* Tenth Anniversary Expanded Edition (Sisters, Oreg.: Multnomah, 1996), pp. 168-169.

17. 2 Corinthians 9:11.

18. C. S. Lewis, *Mere Christianity* (New York: Macmillan), p. 86.

CHAPTER THREE

1. See Matthew 24:35.

2. http://www.chron.com/cs/CDA/story.hts/special/enron/1178373

3. http://www.salon.com/tech/feature/2002/01/23/enron_toll/

4. http://www.salon.com/tech/feature/2002/01/23/enron_toll/

5. http://www.salon.com/tech/feature/2002/01/23/enron_toll/index1.html

6. brookings.edu/views/papers/graham/20020722.htm

7. http://thedoormagazine.com/presslink/Lay_Interview_online.pdf

8. See James 2:26.

9. http://www.texasbusiness.org/legends/index.html

10. http://thedoormagazine.com/presslink/Lay_Interview_online.pdf.

11. Mark 12:43-44.

12. http://www.businessweek.com/bwdaily/dnflash/aug2001/
nf20010824_288.htm

13. Brian Cruver, *Anatomy of Greed* (New York: Carroll and Graf, 2002), p. 135.

CHAPTER FOUR

1. Susan Tosoni, interview by author, 20 September 2002. Undisclosed Enron source, interview by author, 16 September 2002.

2. Dallas Willard, *The Divine Conspiracy* (San Francisco: HarperSanFrancisco, 1998), p. 308.

3. Patrick M. Lenciani, "Make Your Values Mean Something," *Harvard Business Review*, July 2000, p. 113.

4. See, for example, 1 Corinthians 10:3; 1 John 2:15; 1 Peter 2:11.

5. Moses Maimonides, n.d.

6. Desmond Tutu, "The Divine Imperative," *The Rainbow People of God* (New York: Doubleday, 1994), p. 70.

7. Galatians 5:20, MSG.

8. Bryan Magee, *The Story of Thought* (London: DK Publishing, 1998), pp. 92-93.

9. Titus 1:16, MSG.

10. Acts 26:20, emphasis added.

11. Tutu, p. 71.

12. Ruth 4:7, MSG.

13. Colossians 3:23-25, MSG.

14. Micah 7:1-7, MSG.

15. Tutu, p. 71.

CHAPTER FIVE

1. http://systemnews.cdsinc.com/system-news/jobdir/submitted/2001.07/3669/3669.html

2. http://pub42.ezboard.com/fabundantlivinginvestmentsfinance.show Message?topicID=485.topic

3. Wendy Zellner, Christopher Palmeri, Mike France, Joseph Weber, and Dan Carney, *BusinessWeek*, 11 February 2001.

4. Zellner.

5. Zellner.

6. http://pub42.ezboard.com/fabundantlivinginvestmentsfinance.show Message?topicID=485.topic

7. http://pub42.ezboard.com/fabundantlivinginvestmentsfinance.show Message?topicID=485.topic

8. http://news.bbc.co.uk/hi/english/static/in_depth/business/2002/enron/4.stm

9. http://www.soulcare.org/survival_of_the_coolest.htm

10. Proverbs 16:18, MSG.
11. Proverbs 29:23, MSG.
12. Leviticus 26:19, MSG.
13. 2 Corinthians 5:10.

CHAPTER SIX

1. http://www.josephsoninstitute.org/quotes/quotevanity.htm
2. http://www.themediadrome.com/content/articles/words_articles/Quotes/pride.htm
3. http://www.wetfeet.com/employer/articles/article.asp?aid=534
4. Ann Joyner, interview by author, 16 September 2002.
5. http://www.josephsoninstitute.org/quotes/quotevanity.htm
6. *Houston Chronicle*, November 11, 2002.
7. 1 John 2:16, MSG.
8. Martin Luther, *The Large Catechism* (Indypublish.com), p. 109.
9. C. S. Lewis, *Mere Christianity* (Westwood, New Jersey: Barbour and Company, Inc.), pp. 102-103.
10. Lewis, pp. 104-105.
11. Richard J. Foster, *Celebration of Discipline: The Path to Spiritual Growth* (San Francisco: HarperSanFrancisco, 1978, 1988, 1998), p. 130.
12. Foster, p. 66.
13. Foster, p. 66.
14. Matthew 23:12, MSG.

CHAPTER SEVEN

1. http://www.indianexpress.com/ie/daily/19990307/iex07013.html
2. Robert Bryce, "Diva of the Deal," *Houston Press*, 10-16 October 2002, Volume 14, Number 41 (from *Pipe Dreams: Greed, Ego, and the Death of Enron* by Robert Bryce), p. 31.
3. http://www.indianexpress.com/ie/daily/19990307/iex07013.html
4. Bryce, p. 31.
5. http://www.indianexpress.com/ie/daily/19990307/iex07013.html
6. http://www.indianexpress.com/ie/daily/19990307/iex07013.html
7. Bryce, p. 31.
8. Brian Cruver, *Anatomy of Greed* (New York: Carroll & Graf, 2002), p. 102.
9. http://www.indianexpress.com/ie/daily/19990307/iex07013.html
10. http://www.bizjournals.com/houston/stories/2000/10/23/daily31.html
11. Marie Brenner, "The Enron Wars," *Vanity Fair*, April 2002, p. 202.

12. Brenner, p. 202.

CHAPTER EIGHT

1. Peter Behr and April Witt, "Visionary's Dream Led to Risky Business," *Washington Post*, 28 July 2002, A1.
2. Robert Bryce, "Diva of the Deal," *Houston Press*, October 10-16, 2002, Volume 14, Number 41 (from *Pipe Dreams: Greed, Ego, and the Death of Enron* by Robert Bryce), p. 31.
3. Jack Beatty, "The Enron Ponzi Scheme,"*Atlantic Unbound*, 13 March 2002.
4. Michael King, "Enron's Masters of the Universe," *Austin Chronicle*, 4 October 2002, p. 23.
5. Desmond Tutu, "The Divine Imperative," *The Rainbow People of God* (New York: Doubleday, 1994), p. 72.
6. Genesis 47ff.
7. See, for example, King Solomon's musings in the book of Ecclesiastes, or the story of Athaliah in 2 Kings 11.
8. See Genesis 3:5.
9. Proverbs 25:2, MSG.
10. Mark 10:42, MSG.
11. Proverbs 31:4-5, MSG.
12. Deuteronomy 17:19, MSG.
13. Acts 20:35, MSG.

CHAPTER NINE

1. http://www.cfo.com/Article?article=1337
2. http://www.cfo.com/article/1,5309,7805|||9,00.html
3. http://www.time.com/time/business/article/0,8599,201871,00.html
4. http://www.time.com/time/business/article/0,8599,201871,00.html
5. Marie Brenner, "The Enron Wars," *Vanity Fair*, April 2002, p. 195.
6. Mary Flood, "Fastow Pleads Not Guilty to 78-Count Indictment," *Houston Chronicle*, 7 November 2002.
7. Peter Behr and April Witt, "Concerns Grow Amid Conflicts," *The Washington Post*, 30 July 2002, A01+.
8. Psalm 78:30, MSG.
9. Matthew 6:23, MSG.
10. Jack Beatty, "The Enron Ponzi Scheme," *Atlantic Unbound*, March 13, 2002.
11. 1 John 2:16, MSG.

12. See Mark 8:36.
13. Brian Cruver, *Anatomy of Greed* (New York: Carroll & Graff, 2002), p. 337.
14. Cruver, p. 127.

CHAPTER TEN

1. April Witt and Peter Behr, "Losses, Conflicts Threaten Survival," *Washington Post*, 31 July 2002, A01+.
2. April Witt and Peter Behr, "Dream Job Turns into a Nightmare," *Washington Post*, 29 July 2002, A01+.
3. That is, no one has been proven guilty as of November 2002.
4. Enron Values Statement, internal document.
5. Matthew 7:20.
6. Martin Luther King Jr. "Letter from a Birmingham Jail," *I Have A Dream* (New York: HarperCollins), p. 92.
7. Jack Beatty, "The Enron Ponzi Scheme," *Atlantic Unbound*, 13 March 2002.
8. http://www.msnbc.com/news/793737.asp
9. www.motherjones.com/web_exclusives/features/news/enron_insure.html
10. Jeremiah 12:1.
11. See, for example, Psalm 73.
12. Proverbs 13:22.
13. Psalm 90:4, MSG.
14. Hebrews 13:5-6, MSG.
15. *The Essential Rumi*, Trans. Coleman Barks (New York, HarperCollins), pp. 168-69.
16. Psalm 27:14; Psalm 46:10.
17. Stanley M. Hauerwas and William H. Willimon, *The Truth About God: The Ten Commandments in Christian Life* (Nashville: Abingdon Press, 1999).
18. Matthew 6:26, MSG.
19. See 1 Corinthians 9:24,27; Philippians 3:14; Colossians 2:18.

CHAPTER ELEVEN

1. Sherron Watkins to Ken Lay, memorandum, 15 August 2001.
2. Sherron Watkins to Ken Lay, memorandum, 15 August 2001.
3. http://www.nawbook.org/html/about_sherron_watkins.html
4. Sherron Watkins to Ken Lay, memorandum, 15 August 2001.
5. http://www.guardian.co.uk/enron/story/0,11337,640205,00.html

6. http://www.time.com/time/pow/article/0,8599,194927,00.html

7. http://www.forbes.com/home/2002/02/14/0214watkins.html

8. http://www.guardian.co.uk/enron/story/0,11337,640205,00.html

9. Hebrews 12: 1-3.

10. Sherron Watkins, lecture Salem Lutheran Church, Tombal, Texas, 18 October, 2002.

11. http://friendshipbc.com/stories/sherron_watkins_and_enron/story_sherron_watkins_and_enron.htm

12. http://www.dailycelebrations.com/111001.htm

13. http://www.dailycelebrations.com/111001.htm

14. April Witt and Peter Behr, "Losses, Conflicts Threaten Survival," *Washington Post*, 31 July 2002, A1+.

15. Sherron Watkins to Ken Lay, memorandum, 15 August 2001.

CHAPTER TWELVE

1. Jack Beatty, "The Enron Ponzi Scheme," *Atlantic Online*, 13 March 2002.

2. 2 Thessalonians 3:10.

3. Brian Cruver, *Anatomy of Greed* (New York: Carroll & Graf, 2002), p. xii.

4. Isaiah 56:11, MSG.

5. 2 Corinthians 8:14, MSG.

6. "Color-Blinded," *Christianity Today*, 2 October 2000.

7. Michael King, "Enron's Masters of the Universe," *Austin Chronicle*, 4 October 2002, p. 23.

8. Stanley M. Hauerwas and William H. Willimon, *The Truth About God: The Ten Commandments in Christian Life* (Nashville: Abingdon Press, 1999), p. 109.

9. Michael King, "Enron's Masters of the Universe," *The Austin Chronicle*, 4 October 2002, p. 23.

10. Stanley Hauerwas, "What Would Pope Stanley Say," *Christianity Today*, November/December 1998, Vol. 4, No. 6, p. 16.

11. Acts 4:32.

12. Genesis 2:18.

13. Isaiah 5:8.

14. Desmond Tutu, "Apartheid's 'Final Solution,'" *The Rainbow People of God* (New York: William Morrow, 1994), p. 93.

15. Philippians 2:21, MSG.

16. Philippians 2:7.

CHAPTER THIRTEEN

1. http://www.wsws.org/articles/2002/jan2002/enro-j28.shtml
2. http://www.wsws.org/articles/2002/jan2002/enro-j28.shtml
3. http://news.bbc.co.uk/1/hi/business/1784945.stm
4. http://news.bbc.co.uk/1/hi/business/1784945.stm
5. http://news.bbc.co.uk/1/hi/business/1784945.stm
6. http://www.enron.com/corp/pressroom/releases/2001/ene/41-CliffBaxter-05-02-01-LTR.html
7. Fusaro and Miller, *What Went Wrong at Enron* (Hoboken, New Jersey: John Wiley & Sons, Inc., 2002), p. 112.
8. Psalm 89:47.
9. Psalm 39:4-6.

CHAPTER FOURTEEN

1. Matthew 6:33; Matthew 22:37; James 1:8; Matthew 6:24 (KJV).

CHAPTER FIFTEEN

1. John 8:7.
2. John 8:11.
3. Micah 3:1, MSG.
4. Micah 6:9-16, MSG.
5. http://www.umns.umc.org/News97/dec/704.htm
6. http://www.thebody.com/index.shtml
7. http://www.warmblankets.org/crisis.asp
8. http://salt.claretianpubs.org/stats/homeless/home.html
9. *Sojourner* magazine, n.d.
10. Bread for the World, quoting *BusinessWeek* and *The Washington Post*.
11. http://salt.claretianpubs.org/stats/misc/miscsta.html
12. Micah 6:7-8, MSG.

CHAPTER SIXTEEN

1. http://www.pbs.org/kcts/affluenza/
2. Luke 12:15, MSG.
3. 2 Corinthians 8:13-15.
4. *Brickyard Road*, April 2002.
5. Hebrews 13:5.
6. Psalm 131:1-2, MSG.

7. John Piper, *Desiring God,* Tenth Anniversary Edition (Sisters, Oreg.: Multnomah, 1996), pp. 162-163.
8. Matthew 6:24, 31-32, NLT.
9. 1 Timothy 6:9-10, NLT.
10. Mark Buchanan, Consumer Essay Contest, www.christianitytoday.com.
11. Peter Gomes, *The Good Book* (New York: William Morrow, 1996), p. 300.
12. Amos 5:24, NASB.

EPILOGUE
1. James 1:17.
2. Romans 4:4, MSG.
3. http://thedoormagazine.com/presslink/Lay_Interview_online.pdf
4. Sherron Watkins, lecture at Zion Lutheran Church, Tomball, Texas, 18 October 2002.
5. http://thedoormagazine.com/presslink/Lay_Interview_online.pdf
6. Hebrews 13:5-6, MSG.
7. Proverbs 22 (paraphrased).

AFTERWORD
1. David Wells, *God in the Wasteland* (Eerdmans, 1994), p. 114.
2. Romans 1:16.
3. http://trinitycovenant.home.att.net/popepaper.html#_Toc517446622
4. See Luke 14:28.
5. Richard Halverson, chaplain of the United States Senate, quoted by Leighton Ford, *Transforming Leadership*, pp. 163-164.
6. http://trinitycovenant.home.att.net/popepaper.html#_Toc517446622
7. http://trinitycovenant.home.att.net/popepaper.html#_Toc517446622
8. http://trinitycovenant.home.att.net/popepaper.html#_Toc517446622

APPENDIX
1. 1 Corinthians 6:12.

Chris Seay is pastor of Ecclesia, a progressive Christian community in Houston, Texas, recognized for exploring spiritual questions of culture and breaking new ground in art, music, and film. He travels extensively speaking on faith and postmodernity. Seay, author of *The Gospel According to Tony Soprano* and a contributor to *Stories of Emergence*, has appeared on numerous radio and television broadcasts, including CNN and ABC News. His books have been reviewed in *USA Today*, *Entertainment Weekly*, and *Publisher's Weekly*.

Chris Bryan was vice president of administration and human resources for Enron Oil and Gas Company from 1984 to 1997, having left the position to pursue a life of service in Christian ministry. Currently, Chris is interim administrator for Baptist Mission Centers and recently served as associate pastor at Baptist Temple Church in Houston, Texas. Chris received a bachelor's degree in personnel management from Texas Tech University and an M.Div. degree from George W. Truett Seminary at Baylor University. He and his wife, Judy, live in Houston and are the parents of two daughters, Heather and Amy.